ANSWERS
to
Your
Questions

REV. RICHARD V. LAWLOR, S.J.

St. Paul Editions

IMPRIMI POTEST:
    Edward M. O'Flaherty, S.J.
    Provincial, New England Province

NIHIL OBSTAT:
    Rev. Msgr. Matthew P. Stapleton, S.J.
    Censor Deputatus

IMPRIMATUR:
    + Humberto Cardinal Medeiros
    Archbishop of Boston

Library of Congress Cataloging in Publication Data

Lawlor, Richard V.
    Answers to your questions.

    1. Catholic Church—Doctrinal and controversial works—
Catholic authors—Miscellanea. 2. Christian ethics—Catholic authors—
Miscellanea. I. Title.
BX1754.3.L38   230'.2   79-14538

ISBN 0-8198-0700-1 cloth
ISBN 0-8198-0701-X paper

Printed in U.S.A. by the Daughters of St. Paul
50 St. Paul's Ave., Boston, Ma. 02130

The Daughters of St. Paul are an international congregation of religious women serving the Church with the communications media.

INTRODUCTION

There is no problem that faith cannot solve, no question that truth cannot answer. This timely volume contains inquiries sent in by readers of *The Family* magazine over a period of several years.

Covering topics such as prayer, morals, doctrine, marriage, ethics, and the Bible, a competent theologian provides in a concise but clear manner answers to *your* questions. This book is a helpful guide in confronting the prominent issues of our day—a book of answers in an age of questioning.

The Daughters of St. Paul

CONTENTS

MARRIAGE

DOCTRINE

ETHICS

MISCELLANEOUS

MARRIAGE

WHAT CAN I TELL HIM?

Dear Father,

Since I have been receiving "The Family" magazine I have been really impressed by your answers in the "Letter of the Month" column. I decided to write since I am a bit embarrassed to ask a priest about my problem.

My religion means a great deal to me. About two years ago I married a divorced man who has three children. I was not the cause of the divorce, which he obtained six years before I met him.

Before we married (by a judge), we went to talk to a priest-friend who was my pastor at the time. My husband was told by the priest that he had "exceptional" evidence (the priest knew him and the circumstances of the marriage) to obtain an annulment. (He married her because she was pregnant with his child and shortly after, she displayed exceptional mental disorders for which she received extensive treatment.)

The crux of the matter is that now my husband refuses to try to obtain the annulment, saying that he does not want to make his children illegitimate.

Father, please advise me on the Church's teaching in this regard. We love each other and the children and try to lead good Christian lives, although we cannot receive Holy Communion. I know my husband loves his children dearly and he thinks that this annulment would mean that he does not care for them.

What can I tell him? Should I press on for him to begin his petition annulling the first marriage? Or should I let things go as they are?
Grateful for Advice

Dear Grateful for Advice,
The two of you seem to be struggling with a non-problem, and that should make it easier to handle. Let me set down some of the pertinent data:

Legitimacy is the standing of a child before the law, either civil or ecclesiastical. These children are legitimate by both civil and ecclesiastical law, but let me talk only of the latter:

1. If the child was conceived or born of a valid marriage, clearly there is no problem.

2. A child is also legitimate if it was conceived or born of a putative marriage, i.e., an invalid marriage celebrated duly in the Church with good faith by at least one of the parties. In other words, a putative marriage is one that isn't valid but has the appearance of being so.

3. A child conceived outside marriage but born after the marriage is legitimate.

It seems quite clear that all three children are legitimate. If so, nothing anyone can say or do will change that fact. If the first marriage was invalid (putative, in this case), then you should move quickly to have it so declared and then regularize your own situation.

Your priest-friend says that there are "exceptional" grounds to find the prior marriage null. Why hesitate? You have a serious obligation to act. The problem really seems to boil down to this: in a mistaken desire to help the children, the two of you are hurting both them and yourselves by continuing to live in a bad marriage. What sense does that make?

Don't be embarrassed to ask a priest about this problem. That's what priests are for. No priest ordained even a few months will be scandalized; he will simply be happy to help you.

Briefly, the desire not to hurt the children is much ado about nothing. The problem is not their legitimacy, but the sad fact that you are living now in an invalid marriage. Don't waste another moment. See to it that your state before God is so regularized that you will have the right once again to go to Holy Communion. That is the way really to live a good Christian life.

(September, 1974)

"MY HUSBAND AND I BOTH AGREED..."

Dear Father,

I have three children, one is four, the other is two, and the youngest is just five weeks old.

My husband and I both agreed that we don't want any more children right now because of the high cost of living—especially food—which keeps rising every day.

How can we go about this without committing a mortal sin? I would appreciate it greatly if you would answer my letter as soon as possible.

A young mother

Dear young mother,

I can appreciate the difficulty you and your husband face. It is good to see that you want to follow God's law when so many people today, including Catholics, follow their own wills, and not God's. The will of God as the Church spells it out for us is not always easy to follow. It can demand great sacrifice and self-denial.

Vatican II taught that although marriage and conjugal love are by their nature ordained toward the begetting and education of children, some circumstances will indicate that pregnancies should be avoided temporarily or, in some rather rare cases, permanently. The parents make their judgment honestly before

God, and then, in regard to the methods of limiting family size, "...spouses should be aware that they cannot proceed arbitrarily. They must always be governed according to a conscience dutifully conformed to the divine law itself, and should be submissive towards the Church's teaching office, which authentically interprets that law in the light of the gospel" (Vatican II, Church in the Modern World, n. 50).

Pope Paul VI in *Humanae vitae* reiterated the unchanging teaching of the Church that contraception is always grave matter. It is no secret that many Catholics and even some priests reject this teaching. They are wrong. Any Catholic or any priest who says that artificial contraception is permitted is in serious error. Their false views cannot be followed. The test of truth is quite simple: what does the magisterium of the Church (the Pope and the bishops in union with him) have to say? They say quite clearly and flatly that contraception is always wrong. Here is a brief summary of Church teaching as it touches your problem:

1. Parents have a right to decide, as you have, that at this time another child would be too difficult.

2. The means they use to avoid another pregnancy must be morally acceptable. Hence contraception, which aims at spoiling a marital act that might otherwise bring about conception, is forbidden as seriously wrong.

3. Moral means of avoiding pregnancy are:

a. total abstinence from marital relations.

b. periodic abstinence, which is called "Natural Family Planning."

Total abstinence, while not impossible with the grace of God, is obviously quite difficult. For most people Natural Family Planning is the moral means they will want to follow. Natural Family Planning is also difficult, since it restricts the days open to marital intercourse, but thousands of Catholics, under God's grace, have followed the Natural Family Planning method and in so doing kept the law of God.

Get in touch with a good priest who can tell you where to go for information on Natural Family Planning. Some Catholic doctors can help and certainly the Family Life Bureau, if your diocese has one, will know just what to tell you.

Every blessing to you and your family. Stay close to our Lord and He will never, never abandon you.

(October, 1974)

"SHOULD WE STEER CLEAR OF THEM?"

Dear Father,

We enjoy The Family *magazine very much and included in that is the "Letter of the Month." I never thought I'd have to write anyone to find consolation and a few answers to many questions, but here I am and very much distressed over what we have run into the last several months.*

In the past three days alone, we have attended functions and classes of various sorts and have entered into light discussions. One of the first things said is, "I hate children. Who needs them?, etc.," and then all the reasons why they personally can't stand the little people. Sure, down to the last one, they're all selfish reasons. Most, but not all these people, have been divorced at least once.

Along with all this, we must listen to the various means of prevention of birth. And, Father, I find men are no different from women in these matters.

What disturbs me the most is that these people will then proceed to say they are Christians, they are Catholics, and they receive the sacraments daily in some cases.

My question is: how does one react to this? What can you say and still maintain a degree of friendship? Or should a person just steer clear of people who are of this mind? Is it possible that this is a Christian idea and that we are wrong in considering it wrong thinking?

It seems to me that this kind of thinking is taking over very rapidly, and it is disturbing to us.

And may I add, Father, that if our thinking is correct, we find no consolation in our much-loved Church—at least not at the local level.

My husband and I depend on Jesus to continue to give us strength to keep our chin up. May we never lose sight of Him!

Thanks much for listening and any advice and encouragement you can give will be appreciated.

A lover of children

Dear lover of children,

There are, sad to say, people who hate children. And many of them boldly proclaim their feelings and try to justify them. The reasons are selfish, and almost always they are tied to a contraceptive mentality. A child (unwanted) is either a sign that birth control didn't work or else a sign that somebody (horrors!) isn't practicing birth control. Obviously, to people of this stamp, a child is not a beloved sign of a fruitful marital love.

Such people rapidly take to defending premarital sex, abortion, euthanasia and easy divorce. Catholics (including priests) who disputed *Humanae Vitae* are moving in the same direction. Pope Paul VI was well aware of this; he knew that it all hangs together. Either you respect God's law as it is written in human nature and revelation, or you tear the fabric of society apart.

And that is just what is happening. We now have Catholics who say that valid marriages can be dissolved and moralists who say that a thou-shalt-not commandment is not really universally binding but only an ideal which God proposes, but which we need never really attain. We *should* be pure, of course; we *should* be monogamous; we *should not* kill the elderly or unborn babies, but if we do any of these things, the new moralists will forgive us rather easily, since no one can expect us to do more than take a stab at such high ideals. In other words, if a law is very, very hard, it need not be kept, they say.

You are not wrong in thinking that this is wrong thinking. These Catholics are wrong and they cannot be followed. Listen to the magisterium—the Pope and the bishops in communion with him. There you will find the Church's true teaching, not from dissident priests or misguided Catholics.

It may seem odd that such Catholics go to Communion often. But any sinner, no matter how bad, if he is truly sorry for his sins and has a firm purpose of amendment, may have his sins forgiven and then receive Holy Communion. In fact, he should, because he needs grace badly. But if, for example, he flouts the Church's teaching on birth control and has no intention of mending his (or her) ways, then no priest in the world has the right to give him absolution. If the priest does absolve such persons, despite their seriously defective dispositions, the absolution is invalid and their sins are not forgiven.

It is true that more and more Catholics are accepting wrong and twisted thinking. But if they are wrong, they are wrong. In my opinion, their stubborn resistance to the truth has greatly weakened their faith and, as a consequence, they are unable to see and think straight about many issues. The birth controller soon wants the Church to accept divorce. The contraceptive divorcee hates children. In brief, the Catholic sense of these people has been so eroded that some of them will lose the Faith entirely and some will hand on a weak faith to their children.

Don't give up on them. They are pitiful and need our help. Do what you can, if possible, to defend the truth, but keep their friendship. Try to be kindly, but be firm. Friendship does not demand that we deny the truth.

If you do not get support locally, turn to our Lord with greater urgency. He will never abandon you, even if His unworthy children do so. Do not allow the sins of men to obscure in your heart the unfailing love of God. He loves us and He loves His Church—warts and all.

(February, 1975)

"I HAVE DEEP GUILT FEELINGS..."

Dear Father,

I am a fallen-away Catholic, confused and attending my husband's church. Before he met me he married at age seventeen because his girl was pregnant. When the baby was born, his wife started to run around with another man. She asked for a divorce and he gave it to her. His ex-wife has proved to be a loose woman.

A year ago I married this man, whom I love very much. I know the Church would say we are living in sin and I have deep guilt feelings because I was brought up a good Catholic. I love God but am torn apart inside.

When we tried to fix up our marriage we were told to try for the Pauline Privilege or else to pay for an investigation of the previous marriage to see if it was valid. That would be a waste of time because my husband has no close friends who knew him when he was married to her, and she would be very uncooperative and would not admit anything. Besides, we can't afford an investigation.

What do I have to do to clear my mind and live in God's good graces? How do I know that I am doing the right thing by joining my hus-

band's church? Or should I still go to the Catholic Church even though I can't receive the sacraments?

Confused and Guilty

Dear Confused and Guilty,

I wish I could explain and settle your marriage situation in a couple of paragraphs, but I can't. However, I urge you to write or call the chancery for an appointment. Don't worry about expenses. Chanceries, I assure you, are not money-making enterprises. Once you have explained your situation they will be able to tell you what perhaps can be done to regularize your marriage.

It is obvious from the way your letter reads that your conscience is very uneasy. An uneasy conscience is a painful thing, but if it didn't hurt we would not know that we were sick. God is speaking to your heart, gently but firmly telling you to listen.

So come home to your mother, the Church. And go with confidence to the chancery to explain your problem. I am sure you will get help and good advice. The all-important thing is always to find God's will and to follow it. You will not find His will, or follow it, outside the Church. Even though you can't receive the sacraments at present, come back to your own Church. By God's mercy, you belong there, and may you, by God's mercy, find there a solution to your distressing problem.

(January, 1976)

DIALOGUE IS CALLED FOR

Dear Father,

My brother has been away from the Church for some years; he would now like to come back and bring his three sons, ages seven, five and three.

His problem is that he is married to a non-Catholic who believes in God, but not in going to church.

How will this affect him? What can I tell him?

Thank you,
"His Sister"

Dear Sister,

The first answer I want to give is, "Welcome home, brother!"

The second is, "Let's work this out with the help of God, mutual forbearance and patience."

Since charity begins at home, your brother should first of all return quickly to holy Mother Church. His obligation to care for his own soul is primary. Now for his simultaneous obligations to his wife and children:

A Catholic in a mixed marriage is obliged to keep his own Catholic faith intact and to see to it, as far as possible, that his children are brought up Catholics. The problem is that the non-Catholic parent also has obligations towards the children, and that a parent's conscience must be respected. Obviously, this is one of the most serious difficulties of a mixed marriage. I presume that your brother's wife knows—as she surely does if they were married in the Church—her husband's obligations to the children in this regard.

How can two differing consciences be followed? There is no simple answer. Your brother should return to his Church and the sacraments, consult a priest and then, without disrupting his marriage, see if anything can be done to change his wife's mind. Even if, ultimately, he cannot now bring his sons into the Church, his conscience will be clear because he both cared for his own soul by returning to the Church and tried to share that blessing with his children.

Since his wife believes in God, surely she can be persuaded that her sons will not be harmed by a similar belief shared with the members of the largest Church in Christendom. Should she not be willing to give a little, without any conscience compromise, especially since her husband feels so deeply about the spiritual welfare of their boys?

In other words, courteous, respectful dialogue is called for. In the long run, if success is not immediate, your brother can give his boys not just a general belief in God but the example of a dedicated Catholic. Prayer and patience are called for, and trust in God our Father. And God bless you, sister, for helping.

(February, 1976)

"CAN I SAVE MY MARRIAGE?"

Dear Father,

After only four years of marriage, my wife has left me. I know that if I give in to what she wants, I will get her back, but my problem is this: to save my marriage, which means everything to me, I must lose all my self-respect. Once I've done that, won't my wife come to think so little of me that eventually she'll walk out for good?

Specifically, what my wife expects is that I keep on supporting her while she earns her master's degree and that I do all the housework, provide her with transportation, entertainment, etc. Lately, she refused even to do a thing in the kitchen and complained that I don't have enough energy to earn a raise so that we can live better. Of course, she doesn't want to hear anything about having children—ever.

When my wife and I met, we were both in college. She was earning good grades, whereas it was always a struggle for me. I finally decided to quit when a good job opportunity came up (my present job). Before our marriage, she was going to have to quit, too, for financial reasons. After our marriage, I encouraged her to continue in college. She only had a year more to go. She did, but only at my urging.

At that time her whole interest was in our marriage. Although not very religious, she had eagerly cooperated in all the preparations for our Church wedding. Our pastor was even impressed by her attitude.

What happened? About a year ago, she became very friendly with a group of women whose ideas she gradually made her own. The result was the situation we're now in.

I honestly don't know what move to make next. Some of my friends say, "Just keep cool and hang in there—she'll be back." But with her mother babying her and her friends filling her head with their ideas, I've got my doubts.

What do you think about our situation, Father? Am I morally obliged to make the sacrifice move to try to save our marriage? Or have you any suggestions for trying to reason things out with her?

Waiting

Dear Waiting,

Your marriage situation is certainly trying. Without too much reading between the lines, I can see that your wife has been influenced by some of the more reprehensible features of the women's liberation movement. She is unreasonable in her demands of you and is neglecting her duties as a wife.

Although I cannot be sure of all the points at issue, from what you say I doubt that your marriage can be salvaged. A wife who leaves her husband in the circumstances you describe seems to be a very difficult life partner.

You say that she wants no children, ever. If the intention from the beginning has been to exclude children permanently by means of artificial contraception, there is no question of the presence of a true Catholic marriage.

I may be wrong, since as always in such matters many questions have to be asked. It is just possible that you may be able to save this marriage. The best—and urgent—advice I can give to you is to consult a priest (or your local chancery). If the marriage has a decent chance of survival, perhaps you will be advised to try to save it. If it is beyond redemption, there is a possibility that you have grounds for a declaration of nullity. In any case, the only sensible thing is to seek competent advice.

I wish all the best for both of you. That may mean reconciliation, or it may mean the end of your life together.

(April, 1976)

TRY TO STRAIGHTEN IT OUT

Dear Father,

This problem concerns my daughter.

Debra married outside of the Catholic Church. Her husband is not Catholic. He was married before at the age of 17 by a Justice of the Peace. His wife was 16 and pregnant. The marriage was dissolved after a short time.

With all the pleading that I did, Debra would not give this young man up. She was married to him by a minister at his home. She is 18, and Richard is 19.

Now my constant worry is: is her soul lost forever? Is there a chance she can get her marriage blessed? She is now expecting—can the baby be baptized even though she may never get to receive Communion?

He (Richard) shows interest in becoming a Catholic.

> *Yours in Christ,*
> *Concerned Mother*

Dear Concerned Mother,

Let me assure you right away that no one's soul is lost forever unless he dies unrepentant in the state of mortal sin. Your daughter is always open to the merciful grace of God, provided only that she is willing to correspond. Her marriage outside the Church is objectively gravely wrong, and she should try to staighten out her situation promptly.

Since Richard shows interest in becoming a Catholic, it should not be too difficult to persuade your daughter to see a priest and explain things. It is at least possible that Richard's first marriage was invalid so that he would be free to marry Debra in the Church. I cannot say that this is so—I merely point out that it is possible, and very much worth investigating.

The baby can be baptized, and should be, if the parents can be expected to raise it as a Catholic. They could give the child no greater gift than baptism and education in the Faith, even if—and I hope this is not so—their own marriage cannot be "blessed."

So do your very best to get the two of them to see a priest. It is a dangerous and unhappy thing to let a bad marriage drag along when decisive action could clear the air. Three souls are involved—mother, father and baby. No one of them need suffer because of procrastination.

(May, 1976)

EXCOMMUNICATION REPEALED

Dear Father,

Since the issue is so important and for many also confusing, could you please clarify again exactly what was meant and what was not meant by the lifting of the excommunication for Catholics who have divorced and remarried?

A reader of The Family

Dear Reader of *The Family*,

Since the Third Council of Baltimore (1884), American Catholics who divorce and remarry have been subject to automatic excommunication.

Excommunication is the most severe of ecclesiastical penalties. It separates the delinquent from the communion of the faithful, most of all from the Holy Eucharist, which is the very heart of that communion. The person excommunicated may not receive the sacraments, may not be a sponsor at Baptism or Confirmation, may not hold Church office, loses any share in the public prayers of the Church, etc. It is important to note that the censure is not imposed simply as a punishment, but is rather a solemn warning to the delinquent that his spiritual condition is perilous and serves as an invitation to penance and reconciliation.

To be liable to excommunication, one must be baptized, delinquent and contumacious, i.e., stubbornly rebellious, so as to have contempt or disregard for the threatened penalty. Not all delinquents, by any means, have this attitude, so they do not incur the excommunication. They are still delinquents and may not receive the sacraments, but at least they are not excommunicated delinquents.

Last May, 1977, the bishops voted to repeal this excommunication, subject to approval by the Holy See. Now Rome's approval has been given. The bishops' intention was to invite these unfortunates to penance and reconciliation, since apparently many of them thought they were beyond help. Most Catholics who divorce and remarry do not intend to leave the Church, but many of them lapse into a kind of quiet despair. The bishops are now urging them to take part in all the activities of the Church that are permitted them. No one is beyond help until and unless he dies impenitent.

The lifting of the excommunication does not mean that divorce and remarriage are now permitted. The Church cannot recognize as valid and sacramental a second marriage after divorce, unless it has been determined that the first marriage was invalid. Nor may those involved now go to confession and Communion as if nothing had happened. Return to full Eucharistic Communion can be permitted only in certain cases. Hence, it is important for all involved in divorce and remarriage to consult a priest or their chancery about their status. A rather surprising number of first marriages are found to be invalid, thus freeing the partners for full return to communion. Even if the first marriage was valid, it is possible, in certain conditions, to permit the partners in the second marriage to continue to stay together. In any case, no matter how hopeless things may seem, the essential thing to do is to check one's status, and to return to whatever degree of communion is possible.

Our society looks upon divorce and remarriage very casually. Catholics are infected also, and easily. The American bishops are now asking us to show compassion and mercy, but not a softness which would deny God's plan for the indissoluble sacrament of Matrimony. Not all tears will be dried, but many can be, and, please God, will be.

(December, 1977)

ANNULMENTS

Dear Father,

Would you please help a very confused person? When and in what cases can a marriage between two baptized persons be annulled? Could you please list for me the cases, if there are any, and the reasons.

Mary Lou of Boston

Dear Mary Lou of Boston:

A Decree of Nullity is a decision by a competent authority (the Diocesan Tribunal) that an apparently valid marriage was actually invalid from the beginning. Many a seemingly valid marriage between two baptized persons can be declared null because of some fatal flaw.

I cannot list all the possibilities, but I can give you a good idea of what can happen.

First, there is the *form* of marriage. This means that, in general, a Catholic must be married before an authorized priest or deacon and two witnesses. If all is not in order, the marriage ceremony may be invalid and the defect must be repaired, if the couple so desires.

Then, there are *impediments* to marriage. A union entered into with an impediment which cannot be dispensed from, such as impotence or a previously valid marriage, is automatically invalid. The same holds for a marriage undertaken without a dispensation from an invalidating impediment open to dispensation, such as marriage with an unbaptized party. This latter marriage could have been valid if the dispensation had been sought and given.

An essential defect in the *consent* to marriage in its true meaning is the most fertile ground for invalidity. When the partners say, "I do," they have to mean it in the way the Church intends. Some people, because of irresponsibility, immaturity (age is not a necessary factor here, since some older people are quite immature), and a host of other factors do not really give themselves unconditionally to each other.

If one or both parties have been forced into the marriage somehow, it is invalid. If one or both place conditions against the very nature of marriage, it is invalid. Examples of this could be the intention never to have children, if parenthood is possible; the intention not to be true and faithful to one's spouse; the intention to break up the marriage if it turns out to be unhappy.

In short, the couple must be able to give the required consent and actually give it. As we know from sad experience, some can't give true consent, and some won't give it. They hedge their self-giving and destroy their marriage before it can begin. They simulate consent, but may be marrying, for example, only for money, or just to give a name to a child conceived out of wedlock and with no intention of permanent commitment.

These flaws, unknown to one or both parties, or concealed by one or the other, make the marriage no marriage from the start. It is the business of Church tribunals to study the case and, where proper, to give a Decree of Nullity —commonly called an annulment.

Some people in unhappy or broken marriages do have just cause for annulment. They should present their case to a priest. If they think they are not being heard sympathetically or with understanding, they should go directly to the Diocesan Tribunal (address in the telephone book). The Church has no desire to break up true marriages, and she cannot. But she is bound to receive mercifully and justly those who somehow have gotten themselves into an apparently valid marriage which was not valid at all. These people have a right to a Declaration of Nullity. If sufficient evidence is presented, they will be given one. Far from being an attack on holy Matrimony, these procedures actually are aimed at a defense of the sacrament of Matrimony itself. It is too holy to be trifled with.

(November, 1978)

DOCTRINE

"WALKING IN THE
FEAR OF THE LORD"

Dear Father,
I can't recall when I last heard a good
"fear sermon" on hell. Why are sermons of this
type avoided?

Sermon Lover

Dear Sermon Lover,

Sermons of this type do seem to be rare these days, and it is more than a pity. I am not suggesting that we revive the objectionable horror homily too common in the past, but we cannot avoid the fact of hell and we should not eliminate fear of the Lord from our Catholic vocabulary. Scripture itself gives us a perfect picture of the proper attitude: "...the Church was in peace and was being built up, walking in the fear of the Lord, and it was filled with the consolation of the Holy Spirit" (Acts 9:31).

We can see from this quotation that the early Church was not hesitant to fear the Lord's judgment, but the fear was not terror. It lived side by side with peace, growth and the interior warmth of consolation. They knew that Christ was their Redeemer, but they also knew that they could reject His salvation and lose their souls. Hence, salutary fear, filial fear. Hell, though real, was not the central doctrine, but it was there and had to be reckoned with.

Some think fear is an unworthy motive, that we should serve God only out of pure, unadulterated love. The truth is that contrition, springing from a motive of fear, is a morally good and supernatural act. The Council of Trent calls it "a gift of God and an inspiration of the Holy Spirit" and "a true and very beneficial sorrow." This fear of the Lord is one of the gifts of the Holy Spirit, a help to assist us to grow in the life of grace.

If we are to fear God out of love instead of loving Him out of fear, as St. Francis de Sales said, we need at least occasional sermons on hell. Christianity should be presented whole and entire; it is not complete without the sad story of sin and possible damnation. I suspect that many priests avoid sermons on this topic because some parishioners would feel that they are too negative and old-fashioned. Truth is never negative or out-of-date. Perhaps part of the neglect flows from a downgrading of the possibility of mortal sin—witness our long Communion lines and empty confessionals. But mortal sin is always possible, and no one, if he wishes to remain a Catholic, should ever convince us otherwise.

So, in the course of a year, parishioners have a right to hear a reasonable presentation

of the whole Faith, with lots of joy and love—
and also fear of the Lord. Perhaps we should
request a revival of parish missions.

(February, 1979)

WHAT ABOUT BAPTISM?

Dear Father,

*It seemed the perfect opportunity for me
to write this letter when I discovered (I am a
subscriber) that* The Family *magazine offers
this service to its readers.*

*I am acquainted with a young woman
(25 years old) who has three children: eight,
five and four. She is a non-Catholic and is
divorced. (So what's new these days!) This
mother has revealed to me that none of her
children were ever baptized. She is not pushing
the matter but has told me that she has no objections to the children's being brought up
Catholic.*

*Although she is willing to convert to
Catholicism, she does not fully understand the
rules and regulations imposed by the Catholic
Church. She is divorced, but does not rule out
the possibility of a second marriage. Since her
first marriage is valid, this would be contrary to
one of the Church's laws.*

*Being a Catholic with a "simple" under-
standing of some of the basic teachings of the
Church, I felt the children should have the*

privilege and opportunity to receive the sacrament of Baptism. The mother's individual status should be irrelevant to the children's individual souls.

My husband and I are practicing Catholics, have no family of our own, and are willing to be the godparents.

Speaking for myself, this was the foundation—a beginning. I could not go any further until the children were baptized. The children have attended Mass with my husband and myself. The eight-year-old would be eligible to receive Communion if he had additional training, which I had planned to initiate and encourage. The boy has taken it upon himself to attend Mass with one of his younger sisters without an accompanying adult.

We, my husband and I, admit there is no sure guarantee that the children would be brought up Catholic. We only have the mother's word and our good intentions.

Looking-for-guidance

Dear Looking-for-guidance,

No one who is capable of Baptism should be refused the chance to be baptized. The Church teaches that baptism of water is necessary for salvation whenever it can be given, but if this is impossible, baptism of desire or blood will suffice.

What about infants who die unbaptized? We simply do not know with certitude, though we can quite reasonably think that God has His own ways, unknown to us, of saving unbaptized infants. But since we are not sure, the Church insists upon the prompt baptism of babies.

The three children you have so kindly taken to your hearts should, in my opinion, be baptized. The mother will have to request their baptism and meet certain requirements. She does not have to become a Catholic herself, although I certainly hope she does. The basic requirement is that she desires and will permit the Catholic upbringing of her children. As godparents, it would be up to you to see to this, and obviously you are the kind of people who can be trusted to do their best.

No "guarantee" is required of the mother, but she must say that she will permit them to be raised as Catholics through you, or, if necessary, others. With the mother's word and your good intentions, I see no reason at all why the children should not be baptized.

So I would urge you to speak to the mother and then to arrange a meeting with any priest of your choice—or perhaps it might be better to begin by finding a priest to perform the baptism and then to speak to the mother. It would be proper, if possible, to go to your own parish church (wherever the children will go to Mass and religion classes) and explain the situation. If at first you don't succeed, go to any Catholic church you choose until you find a priest who will baptize the children. I think it will be easy to find one.

May God bless you for your great goodness, and may He give you in these children another family of your own. If there were more people like you in the world, the Church would be flourishing.

(June, 1974)

"TWO OF OUR CHILDREN HAVE LEFT..."

Dear Father,

This is our problem: Two of our five children have left home because they refuse to accept the authority of their parents regarding (1) dating (2) chastity and (3) dangers of mixed marriages.

In fact, both have informed us that the fourth commandment says "honor," not "obey." This is in addition to many other ideas they have acquired.

What do we do?

Anxious Parents

Dear Anxious Parents,

The ten commandments are lapidary statements, that is, they say very briefly what they mean and imply a great deal more. The implications are spelled out by human reason, the teaching of Scripture and the Church.

Would anyone, for example, be so naive as to say that the commandment not to kill means quite literally that and nothing else—so that it would be morally all right to beat up someone brutally as long as you didn't kill him?

The fourth commandment requires a child to love, reverence and obey his parents. There are many references to this obligation in Sacred Scripture; one that sums it up quite well is this:

> "Children, be obedient to your parents in the Lord—that is your duty. The first commandment that has a promise attached to it is: *Honor your father and mother,* and the promise is: *and you will prosper and have a long life in the land.* And parents, never drive your children to resentment but in bringing them up correct them and guide them as the Lord does" (Eph. 6:1-4).

In other words, children are to obey, and parents must, with loving care, insist that the children know and keep God's law. St. Paul lists disobedience to parents as one of the sins that may be grave (cf. 2 Tim. 3:2; Rom. 1:30). Your two children, if minors and unmarried, had no right to leave home without your permission. They might well reflect upon the fact that Jesus, though God, not only honored His parents, but obeyed them.

Without love and obedience, "honor" becomes an empty word.

The teaching of the Church on chastity is, in itself, quite clear. The difficulty today, as most parents know, lies in the fact that (1) society in general has become permissive about sexual sin to a frightening degree, and (2) some misguided souls seem to be teaching sexual norms that are false or misleading.

Let us hope that your children will come home and bring some peace to your sad hearts. Be generous in forgiving their waywardness and try, with the near-infinite patience God often asks of parents, to lead them in His ways.

If they will not come home, keep praying and keep your door and your hearts always open to them.

(November, 1974)

THE MARLBORO CASE

Dear Father,

I am a Catholic and a faithful reader of The Family *magazine. Recently much publicity was given to a young woman with a newborn child who was denied the sacrament of Baptism by her parish due to her active participation in pro-abortion views.*

My question is: Why was an innocent child denied Baptism by the parish because of the mother's views? It seems strange to me that, in order to punish the mother, the Church would lose an innocent soul.

This item has been a topic of discussion— with various opinions—in our office since it was published in the newspapers. We would appreciate an explanation to settle our dispute on the above subject. Thank you.

Sincerely,
Secretaries

Dear Secretaries,

A great deal of print was expended on the "Marlboro Case," some of it inaccurate and even irresponsible. Let's see if we can outline the essentials, though it must be admitted that a book would be necessary to say all that might be said.

First, it must be stated emphatically that the Church has no desire to punish anybody, nor does she wish to lose an innocent soul. Quite the contrary. The good of souls is what she has in mind from start to finish.

Parents have a serious obligation to have their children baptized rather soon after birth. Baptism should include an expression of faith, but since this is beyond the powers of an infant, the faith is that of the community and especially that of the parents. We must have evidence

from the parents' faith that the Catholic upbringing of the child will be provided for. It is
necessary to realize that the Church does not
demand that the parents be saints or fervent
Catholics, but the faith held and lived by the
parents, poor as it may be, must be the
Catholic Faith, not some private or distorted
version of it. The fact that the parents hold
wrong views cannot be justified by saying that
they have a right to follow their own consciences. No Catholic can follow his private
views if they go against the teaching of the
Church.

Obviously, even parents who are great sinners can profess the full Catholic Faith and
want to hand it on to their children. There is no
trouble about baptizing such children. But
there are cases—and they differ from time to
time and from place to place—where the
Catholic Faith of the parents is so deficient that
the pastor may decide that there is not enough
hope that the baby will be brought up as a real
Catholic. It is very hard to make such a decision, and sometimes the priest may be wrong.

Nonetheless, in doubtful cases someone
must make the hard, practical decision as to
whether or not the future Catholic upbringing of
the child is sufficiently provided for. It is the
pastor's business to make this decision according to the Church's norms and, in particular,
the norms established by the bishop. The priest

in the "Marlboro Case" made his anguished decision, and he was fully supported by his Cardinal Archbishop.

The priest's next step is to try to bring the parents to see and accept the true Catholic Faith; then the postponed baptism may take place. If the parents refuse to amend their ways or their thinking, then the denial of baptism is their own fault. They are the ones who refuse the most basic of the sacraments to their child. There is a good deal of irresponsible talk these days that infant baptism is not really necessary, but there has been no change in the Church's teaching. Infant baptism is still mandatory and necessary. Those who deny it to their children through their own sinfulness have a very great burden on their consciences.

The Church is not trying to whittle her membership down to an elite of the perfect. She is the Church of sinners, great and small, and she loves every one of them. But she cannot trifle with truth. Membership in the Church, which is brought about by Baptism, is a tremendous gift and a weighty obligation. It is not just a social inscription in a club. The "Marlboro Case," properly understood, should make all of us soberly assess our own commitment to our baptismal obligations. And we can and should pray for everyone involved in this unhappy incident. May it work out to the glory of God and the good of all the souls involved.

(December, 1974)

REINCARNATION?

Dear Father,

In our area there is a growing interest and belief in reincarnation. Due to a lot of publicity given to Oriental mysticism, etc., a lot of people I know, older people as well as the young, are getting very confused and involved in it.

My best friend, a Catholic, and mother of seven, recently told me in conversation that she can't find anything in the Bible or in her Catholic Tradition that rejects the possibility of human reincarnation. "I don't believe that we come back as animals, or anything like that, but I really do think we could be reincarnated. In fact, I was previously probably a very self-centered woman, and that's why I had to come back and have a large family that would demand so much of me."

I really feel sorry for her, and a lot more people like her. As I said, so many people of all different denominations are beginning to believe in reincarnation, and I don't know what to say, but I would like to help.

I am Catholic myself and have my own definite ideas against the possibility of reincarnation. I believe God gives us a life for a purpose, and that it's a once-only chance. (In fact, to me it would seem awfully unrealistic to be able to keep having "second chances": oh well, maybe I'll make it next time!)

*As I said, Father, I have my own strong
convictions, but I just can't find the words or
proofs to support them, though I know there
are good ones both from reason and Faith.
Could you offer any help from biblical sources,
Church teaching and just good sound natural
reasoning?*

Worried

Dear Worried,

One sad feature of our time is the
popularity, even among some Catholics, of
Oriental mysticism. I am not rejecting light or
truth, wherever it may be found, but I am
puzzled that Catholics should think it necessary
to look outside their own tradition, incom-
parably the richest in the world, for inspiration
in these matters.

Your friend is wrong if she thinks there is
nothing in the Bible or Catholicism against
reincarnation. There is plenty.

Reincarnation (often called metempsychosis or transmigration of souls) appeared
centuries ago in India and Greece. Variations
of the belief have been found in most parts of
the world. Basically it teaches that the soul at
death passes into another body. Differing and
more or less elaborate forms of this doctrine exist. The purpose of the soul's passing to other
bodies is purification from guilt. A good life
would merit a better embodiment the next time
around, while a bad life would set one lower on
the scale.

This teaching is flatly contrary to the Faith. It has been condemned, directly or indirectly, time and again in the history of the Church.

Just to touch on some of the doctrines which immediately reject metempsychosis: first, man is already redeemed. His only task is to accept that redemption in the one temporal life he has to lead. Right after death comes judgment; there is no re-cycling in another life on this earth. We die once only, and the soul (eventually to be reunited to the body) lives in the state it has chosen, i.e., heaven or hell, forever.

The whole burden of revealed doctrine is against reincarnation. No Christian can hold it. If you want a few Bible texts (there are many more) see Hebrews 9:27; Luke 16:19-31, 23:43; 2 Corinthians 5:10.

There isn't the slightest rational evidence for metempsychosis. As a theory, it denies the unity of the soul in one human personality and effectively destroys individual, moral responsibility. In addition, a key doctrine of the Faith is the immediate creation of each soul by God.

In brief, reason, the Bible, and the teaching of the Church all reject reincarnation. If we try to learn the wonders of the Faith, we won't be dazzled by old errors.

(May, 1975)

WHY SUNDAY?

Dear Father,

I was reading your article in The Family. *I found it very interesting and have some questions. I have been reading my Bible and want to do the Lord's will also. I believe in all the commandments of God, and by God's grace abide in them.*

In your article you started with Deuteronomy 5:12-14: To remember the Lord's day, the seventh day, Sabbath (which is Saturday). But you mentioned to keep holy Sunday (first day of the week).

I'm sincerely concerned with this because of my love for Jesus, and I want to do what He expects of me. I believe the commandments were written by God's hand and are very sacred. In my observation of the commandments, this is the only one that starts with "Remember," and God was also specific about what day to worship on.

I know most churches keep Sunday holy because of Christ's resurrection on that day, but I have found that the seventh day, Sabbath, was kept over three hundred years after the cross, which means the Apostles died keeping the seventh day Sabbath.

In my searching of the Scriptures, I haven't found anything that suggests a change. Have I overlooked something I should know about? I would appreciate an answer with scriptural evidence of such a change.

I believe the commandments are all equally important, and in the last book of the Bible, the apostle John says (Rev. 14:12): "Here is the patience of the saints; here are they that keep the commandments of God, and the faith of Jesus." I want to be among that group as much as you do. That's why I'm searching for answers. Thank you for your time, and may God send you many blessings.

Sincerely,
A searcher

Dear Friend,

The third commandment tells us to keep holy the Sabbath day. Why, then, did Christians from early times celebrate Sunday? An intriguing question.

The first Christians in Jerusalem kept to many Jewish practices while evolving their own. Thus, it seems that at first they celebrated both the Sabbath and Sunday. But as time went on, and especially after many gentiles were converted, concrete decisions had to be made as to which Jewish practices were to be kept and which abandoned. The ten commandments, for example, were of strict obligation insofar as they spelled out the natural moral law, and so they could not be abrogated by the New Covenant.

The Sabbath, however, despite its place in the third commandment, was not of natural moral law. The basic natural law involved was man's obligation to worship God. The specifying of the Sabbath merely tied down the obligation to a particular day. So the early Church, clear that it had to worship God, decided to do so on Sunday. St. Paul in Colossians 2:16 declared Christians free from the Sabbath obligation at a time when Jewish converts to Christianity were trying to impose Old Testament obligations on New Testament Christians.

We don't know all the reasons for the choice of Sunday, but the basic one seems clearly to have been the fact that Christ rose from the dead on the first day of the week, Sunday. Just as the Sabbath was sacred to the Jews as the day on which God rested after creation, Sunday was sacred to Christians as the day of the *new* creation begun with the resurrection. Sunday is the weekly renewal of the resurrection. It is our weekly Easter.

So it is not accurate to say that the Sabbath was the Christian holyday for three hundred years, or that the Apostles died keeping the Sabbath. We read in Acts 20:7: "And on the first day of the week, when we had met for the breaking of the bread...." And Revelation 1:10 speaks of "the Lord's day," which is Sunday. Colossians 2:16, referred to above, which makes a definitive break with the Sabbath obligation, was written within thirty years or so of our Lord's death and resurrection. It did not take long for Sunday observance to be common and accepted. In fact, so clearly was Sunday accepted very early in the Christian era, that St. Ignatius of Antioch could write early in the second century: "Christians no longer observe the Sabbath but live in the observance of the Lord's day on which our life rose again."

In the last analysis, of course, the scriptural basis for Sunday is found in the powers given to the Apostles and their successors, the bishops, to teach, govern and sanctify. Using these powers, they decided very early that the Sabbath was obsolete, and that the first day of the week, Sunday, was henceforth to be the Lord's day. And so it has been ever since.

(June, 1975)

WOMEN AND THE MINISTRY

Dear Father,
Are women allowed to be lay ministers—reading the Bible and giving Communion?
                                        Likes To Know

Dear Likes To Know,
    At the present time in the United States, women may exercise liturgical offices with the exception of serving at the altar. They can be reader, cantor, leader of singing, commen-

tator, and, where there is a real need (but not otherwise), they may be designated to give out Holy Communion.

So the answer to the question as you put it is "Yes." Perhaps it may be helpful and interesting to outline some of the problems suggested by the word "ministry."

First, it is an ambiguous word. If it refers to some service to help the Church, there is no doubt at all about the admission of women to the ministry. Women have ministered to the needs of their fellow Catholics from the very first days of the Church—and superbly.

In November, 1973, the American bishops decided to ask Rome for permission to create two new official ministries (catechist and minister of music) open to lay men and women. In one U.S. diocese, there were recently some thirty sisters and laywomen working with their priests in pastoral ministry.

However, if by "ministry" you mean the office of deacon or priest, the question is quite different. There is a great deal of agitation, much of it unscholarly and some of it simply vulgar, for the ordination of women to the diaconate and priesthood. A committee of American bishops recently issued a report on the subject, and it is a model of intelligent sobriety. Let me give the highlights of their report and comments stimulated by it.

First, Church law (Canon 968) says that women are not eligible for Orders. Up to now we cannot prove or disprove historically that women were ever ordained deacons. No one knows for sure what the early "deaconesses" really were. One very clear fact, testified to by Scripture, is that our Lord had men only as His Apostles. He did not hesitate to contravene the social customs of His time in other matters, but He never made a woman a priest, not even His Mother.

In addition to what we know from Scripture—and it cannot be lightly dismissed as just the custom of the time and not Divine Revelation—we have Tradition, through which God speaks authoritatively to us. Until modern times, all theologians throughout history have held that one must be a male to be ordained, and they have held this as Divine Revelation, not merely custom. In other words, this could be the clear teaching of the ordinary magisterium of the Church.

I think it safe to say that rather soon there may be an authoritative statement from the Holy See on the subject. And I think it will repeat the same doctrine.*

Does this mean women are inferior? Not at all. It only means that they are different, that God gives them different charisms. We all

* The ancient doctrine was re-affirmed by Rome in October, 1976. The Declaration stated that the Church "...in fidelity to the example of the Lord, does not consider herself authorized to admit women to priestly ordination."

share in the common priesthood of the faithful, and some few of us are chosen to minister to the rest through priestly, sacerdotal service. That charism does not, of itself, make the priest any better than the incomparable women who serve us in the ministries of teaching, healing, charity, etc.

So cheer up, ladies. The sexes are equal, but they are different. Equality does not demand identical functions, as if the ideal for women were to be like males in every way. Among creatures, the male is not the perfect model for all of us; a female is: the Blessed Mother of God, who was not a priest. Can anyone say this makes her a lesser being?

Editor's note: As this issue went to press, a statement was released on the subject by Most Rev. Joseph L. Bernardin, then Head of the National Conference of Catholic Bishops. While declaring that "women are called today to a greater leadership role in the Church," and "their contributions are needed in the decision-making process at the parochial, diocesan, national and universal levels," he reiterated the Church's traditional position on ordination for women: "I am obliged to restate the Church's teaching that women are not to be ordained to the priesthood." Further on in the statement, the Archbishop emphasized the importance of woman's role thus:

"The Church has grown more aware of the variety of ministries open to women; in a very special way they are called to collaborate with all other segments of the Church in the essential work of evangelization."

(November, 1975)

AIMED AT THE COMMON GOOD

Dear Father,

Please explain to me the role of extraordinary ministers, especially in churches like mine where there is no shortage of priests. When I see Holy Communion given to the faithful by housewives, I feel that it is just too much.

A concerned gentleman

Dear Concerned Gentleman,

The Sacred Congregation of the Sacraments has issued norms on extraordinary ministers of Holy Communion. Qualified laypeople may be designated for specific occasions or for extended periods in the absence of a sufficient number of priests, deacons or lawfully instituted acolytes.

There must be an objective pastoral need. The usual case (since not all parishes have deacons or lawfully instituted acolytes) is one in which the priest or priests of the parish cannot manage the crowds of communicants at Sunday Mass, or the large numbers of sick and elderly in private homes, nursing homes and hospitals who long for the consolation of the Holy Eucharist. Without help, Sunday Mass would be unduly prolonged; the sick and elderly might be lucky to receive Communion once a month or so.

These novel (to us) concessions are granted for the spiritual good of the faithful, not for the mere convenience of priests. The need of lay help must be genuine, and priests should never, without reason, exempt themselves from their holy duty as ministers of the Eucharist. Granted this, I think we must be grateful for this permission, since it makes our access to Holy Communion more expeditious, more frequent, and even more reverent. I feel sure, moreover, that the privilege of distributing the Body of the Lord will deepen considerably the spiritual lives of the extraordinary ministers.

Admittedly, the practice can be at least a mild shock to many. The assumption is that only the consecrated hands of a priest should touch the sacred Host. But if our Lord deigns to rest on the tongues of all, clerical and lay, is it not fitting that in cases of reasonable necessity He come to us from lay hands? Unfounded taboos should not keep us from ready access to the Bread of Life.

In short, this is a *good* change. It can be abused and perhaps is, here and there. But on the whole, it helps all of us, priests and parishioners. We should try to adapt ourselves patiently to a concession which is aimed only at the common good. And, if I may say so, some of the most worthy extraordinary ministers of the Eucharist are plain "housewives."

(July-August, 1979)

ARE LATIN MASSES PERMISSIBLE?

Dear Father,
    When I read about Archbishop Lefebvre, I became confused as to whether or not a Latin Mass is permitted these days. Could you enlighten me, Father, on the Church's regulations since Vatican II?

A concerned church-goer

Dear Concerned Church-goer,
    Current Church regulations may be summarized thus: the episcopal conference of each area has the right to determine the language of the Mass. In most cases, this will be the vernacular. They may permit Masses in Latin, according to the revised rite, whenever they judge this pastorally good, for parish Masses with a congregation. Some dioceses in the country permit an occasional Latin Mass, with scriptural readings in English. The usage of your own diocese is the norm.
    Please note that in all cases, whatever language is used, the Mass is the revised one made obligatory in the Church after Vati-

can II. To the best of my knowledge, the old Tridentine Mass of Pius V is allowed nowhere in the Church at public Masses.

At any rate, the current law of the Church allows public Masses in Latin under the circumstances described above, and only then. Archbishop Lefebvre, therefore, is in public disobedience to the Church he professes to serve. The poor man seems to think that he is preserving sound doctrine by rejecting the new liturgy. Whatever his subjective disposition, he is in error. In rejecting his stand, the Holy See is not treating him harshly, for his error is not just a private aberration. It is, fundamentally, a rejection of the teaching authority of the Church. People like the Archbishop, who want at all costs to preserve the old liturgy and the old ways, which they confuse with the unchanging Faith, have no true grasp of tradition. The Church is not a fossil, but a living thing. If this were not so, liturgically speaking we would not be celebrating our current Mass, or even the older Tridentine Mass, but would rather still cling to the primitive Mass as said by the Apostles. As our knowledge of the Faith developed, so did our style of worship. Just as Pius V made the "old" Mass obligatory after the Council of Trent, so Paul VI made the new Mass obligatory after Vatican II. In each case the Church is to be obeyed.

Pope Paul VI has had to rebuke the vagaries of both liberals and conservatives. The ultra-conservatives want nothing changed. The ultra-liberals would change almost anything. Both are wrong, and dangerously so, since liturgical errors are the forerunners of doctrinal error. Liturgy and doctrine are so closely bound together that in practice they cannot be separated.

So let us pray for all who deviate from the Church's law, both those who make their own laws for the liturgy and those who will not accept legitimate change. Here, once again, we can see God's great wisdom in giving His Church a magisterium, a teaching authority. The Pope and the Bishops have made their solemn decisions on liturgical practice. Let us not be taken in by the lawless vulgarities of the ultra-liberals or the rigid antiquarianism of the ultra-conservatives. Let us simply be good Catholics, worshiping God as He wants us to.

(January, 1977)

"YOU WILL NEVER BE HAPPY ANYWHERE ELSE"

Dear Father,

It's been a long time now since I've been to Mass, and when you haven't been for a time it's hard to get back, especially since I'm now confused as to what makes a Church the right one.

Is there such a thing as different churches for different people? I seem to have lost the reasons why I should go to the Catholic Church. How can I straighten out my ideas? Will you help me, please?

A bewildered teenager

Dear Bewildered Teenager,

A reasonably full answer to your question would take up more than all the space of this issue of *The Family*. However, let's do the best we can.

We know from the New Testament that Jesus Christ, the Son of God, founded a Church, built upon Peter, the rock. He commanded Peter and other first leaders of the Church to go and make disciples of all nations, that is, to bring all men into the Church He founded. Christ actually identified Himself with His Apostles: "He who hears you, hears me; and he who rejects you rejects me" (Lk. 10:16).

In other words, it was and is the will of God that His Church was the one meant for all men. He did not establish a vague Christianity with room for all sorts of different, even contradictory, doctrines. There is only one true Church, and it is the Roman Catholic Church. So basic is this in Catholic belief that the recent Vatican Council declared: "Hence they could not be saved who, knowing that the Catholic Church was founded as necessary by God through Christ, would refuse either to enter it, or to remain in it" (*Lumen gentium*, no. 14).

No one, then, who knows that the Catholic Church is the true Church is free to pick another church. In this sense there is no such thing as different churches for different people. But, as we all know, there are many, many people who do not know the Catholic Church, or who do not know that it is the Church founded by Jesus Christ. They can, in clear conscience, love and serve God where they are.

Those of us who, by God's great grace, are Catholics, have no right to abandon the Faith. We know, with the certitude of faith, which flows not from our own wisdom or scholarship, but from God's gift of grace, that we are in the one, true Church. The simplest rule to keep in mind is the centuries-old axiom which says, "Where Peter is, there is the Church"; i.e., to be in full communion with the Church Christ founded, you must be in the Church ruled by Peter's successor, the Pope.

One of the great tragedies of our time is the loss, among many Catholics, of a sense of the necessity of the Church. One church is not as good as another. True ecumenism means that we respect the elements of truth found in other religions and work with all our hearts that we may all be one, but it never denies that we Catholics already possess the essential fullness of truth.

So, hurry back to Mass and the sacraments. You may find it awkward and perhaps hard at first, but the Church is your home, your only spiritual home. You will never be happy anywhere else. I will pray that God will make your homecoming easy, as I know He will.

(February, 1977)

DISTINGUISHING TRUTH FROM ERROR

Dear Father,

I desire to teach the unchangeable doctrine of the Church, but I am faced with attitudes prevalent in my area that essentials have changed. For example, how can I distinguish between what the Church teaches and what some authorities advocate regarding essentials..., following one's conscience..., personal sin..., infallible teaching..., Scripture...?

I feel that the deposit of Faith has not changed and that I am gravely responsible to help preserve it. How may I do this?...

An earnest seeker

Dear Earnest Seeker,

The difficulties you have run into are rather common these days, sad to say. You have my sympathy in your efforts to be a good Catholic, loyal to God and His Church. Let me touch upon the points you raise in your letter.

First, nothing which is essential to the Faith changes. Some things which are not essential, such as the use of Latin in the Mass, can be changed by the proper authorities, but none of the basics have been changed and they never will. Unfortunately, since a number of non-essentials have been changed or modified in recent years, some people have the idea that everything is up for grabs. That is why Pope Paul VI has had to make so many statements reaffirming changeless doctrine. There are rebellious and, in some cases, ignorant people in the Church who have brought endless confusion to other Catholics.

For example, there is the matter of *conscience*. We are all bound to follow our conscience, but this does not mean that we do what we please. Our conscience must be informed. It must try to find out what is true, what is right, and then obey. If the Church teaches us that something is wrong, then no matter what I think, I must obey the Church. Thus, for example, pre-marital sex is always gravely forbidden, even if those who indulge in it are to be married soon. Paul VI just recently stated this unchanging doctrine again, simply because there were people who denied it. There has been no change in this teaching and never will be.

Then there is the question of *personal sin*. Although we are not to judge the state of another's conscience, we can and must hold that if he does something that is forbidden strictly by God's law, then what he did is wrong, no matter what he may think. It is quite true that lack of sufficient reflection or lack of full consent may mitigate responsibility; still the thing he did was gravely forbidden. The person may not be guilty of mortal sin, but the act itself is gravely forbidden.

Those responsible for others, then, are obliged to teach them what is right and wrong. They cannot simply let them do what they please.

One of the worse aberrations of recent times is to demand that only infallible teaching must be followed. Some people say that if the Pope or a General Council have not defined something, then we are free to do as we will. This is rank nonsense. Definitions are rare, but the unchanging teaching of the Church must be obeyed. The fact that pre-marital sex is gravely forbidden has never been formally defined, but there is not the slightest doubt that it is gravely sinful, and the teaching will always be the same. This holds for all sorts of things. It is simply pernicious to hold that the authentic teaching of the Church is not binding unless it is infallibly taught.

Another error is to demand that everything must be clear from the Scriptures. The Bible was never intended to be a textbook spelling out every last doctrine. In addition to God's revelation in Scripture, we have Tradition, which explains through the teaching Church (Pope and Bishops) what is to be believed. It is not obvious from a reading of the New Testament that Holy Orders is restricted by God's will to males, but the Church has always taught this and Paul VI has just reiterated this doctrine. Our Lady's Immaculate Conception and her Assumption are not clear from the Bible, but they are defined doctrines of the Faith, and they were just as true before they were formally defined. In other words, to find God's will, we must go to the teaching Church, the Pope and the Bishops. Ignore and reject anyone who tries to teach you anything else.

Sad to say, even some priests say foolish and false things these days. Don't listen to them. Listen to the Pope and the Bishops and priests who are in communion with them. The great truths of the Faith have not changed and will not change. Do the best you can, in peace of conscience, to hold the truth, to speak it when you have the obligation to do so, and when you can't stop things, simply leave it to God. You won't always succeed, but do the best you can and trust in our Lord. I commend you for your fine Catholic spirit, and I sympathize with you deeply in your difficulties. May God be good to you, as I know He will.

(March, 1977)

WHOM DOES THE HOLY SPIRIT SPEAK TO?

Dear Father,

Does the Holy Spirit speak only through the Pope? Doesn't he also speak through the members of the Church, especially when the majority believe the same thing, for example, that contraception is permissible?

A confused Christian

Dear Confused Christian,

Let me answer your question by referring to just a few of the many statements of Vatican II which treat this matter.

The Holy Spirit can and does speak, in different ways, through all of us and not just the Pope. "United in Christ, they are led by the Holy Spirit in their journey to the kingdom of their Father..." (*Church in the Modern World*, no. 1). The laity should be "...sensitive to the movement of the Holy Spirit..." (*Laity*, no. 29). "...By this sense of faith which is aroused and sustained by the Spirit of truth, God's People accept not the word of men but the very Word of God (cf. 1 Thes. 2:13). It clings without fail to the faith once delivered to the saints (cf. Jude 3), penetrates it more deeply by accurate insights, and applies it more thoroughly to life. All this it does under the lead of a sacred teaching authority to which it loyally defers" (*The Church*, no. 12).

So, every Catholic is led by the Holy Spirit. Does this mean he may follow his own ideas and desires? By no means. Some Catholics, both clerical and lay, "...have been unfaithful to the spirit of God during the course of many centuries" *(Church in the Modern World,* no. 43). In other words, their notions were not inspired by God, because God does not lead to error. "The Holy Spirit...stirs up in their hearts the obedience of faith" *(Missions,* no. 15). It is not a question of what a number of Catholics may think, but of the authentic teaching of the Church.

Where do I find the authentic teaching of the Church? From those who have the most special guidance of the Holy Spirit, the bishops: "By the light of the Holy Spirit, they make that faith clear..." *(The Church,* no. 35).

One of the most famous sections of Vatican II spells it out: "In matters of faith and morals, the bishops speak in the name of Christ and the faithful are to accept their teaching and adhere to it with a religious assent of soul. This religious submission of will and of mind must be shown in a special way to the authentic teaching authority of the Roman Pontiff, even when he is not speaking ex cathedra. That is, it must be shown in such a way that his supreme magisterium is acknowledged with reverence, the judgments made by him are sincerely adhered to, according to his manifest mind and will" *(The Church,* no. 25).

In other words, though the Holy Spirit gives the faithful special gifts, for He "breathes where he wills" (Jn. 3:8), they can be misled, and they "...must act in communion with their brothers in Christ, especially with their pastors. The latter must make a judgment about the true nature and proper use of these gifts, not in order to extinguish the Spirit, but to test all things and hold fast to what is good (cf. 1 Thes. 5:12, 19, 21)" (*Laity*, no. 3).

By now, I hope, your question is answered. The firm and constant teaching of the Church forbids contraception, and those who say it is permissible, no matter how many, do not speak with the voice of the Holy Spirit. They are, rather, unfaithful to the Spirit. God does not contradict Himself. As St. Augustine said, "A man possesses the Holy Spirit to the measure of his love for Christ's Church." Christ's Church, speaking through millions of faithful Catholics, and especially through those who have the special guidance of the Spirit (i.e., Pope and bishops), teach us that contraception is wrong. We cannot reject the authentic teaching of the Church and say that we are led by the Spirit, since "...union with those whom the Holy Spirit has assigned to rule God's Church (cf. Acts 20:28) is an essential element of the Christian apostolate" (*Laity*, no. 23).

(October, 1977)

IS THE QUESTION SETTLED?

Dear Father,

I don't believe that women could ever become priests, but many of my friends do. I don't have the answer to persuade them. I believe, however, that they can become deacons just as any other male deacon.

I would appreciate it if you could give me strong reasons on both points to convince myself and my friends. Thank you.

Anxious for the Ministry

Dear Anxious for the Ministry,

For most of the history of the Church the ordination of women to the priesthood was a non-problem. Some heretics in the early centuries did try to ordain women, but they were quickly condemned. Until very recent times the restriction of the priesthood to males was universally accepted in the Church of both East and West.

The questioning of the unvarying tradition, especially by some Americans, prompted a decision from the Holy See. The unfailing teaching of the Church was repeated: women cannot be validly ordained to the priesthood.

The essential reason for this position is quite simply that Christ so willed it. It is no mere disciplinary decree of the Church. The Church has no choice in the matter. She is simply obeying her Divine Master.

Our Lord did not call any woman to be an Apostle, and this was not because He was conforming to the customs of His time. Our Lord's attitude towards women was quite different from that of His contemporaries. He did not relegate them to the background, but treated them with an equality that astonished and even scandalized His followers. It would not have been surprising, given His attitude, if He had made women His priestly Apostles. He did not.

The apostolic community followed His example. Women were outstanding members of the early Church, and they were recognized as completely equal to men in their status before God. There were priestesses in the pagan world of the time, so the idea of ordination would not have been wholly alien. But there was never any question of ordaining women in the Church.

The practice of Christ and His Apostles has been considered normative for all time. The Church knows that she can never change the essential aspects of a sacrament, and in regard to the priesthood, restriction to males is, by God's will, essential.

The Church would never have dared to deprive women of this great office unless it was the will of Christ that things be so. It might be noted that not only are women excluded from the priesthood, but also the majority of men! Only one called by God and accepted by the Church can be ordained.

The detailed reasons behind this teaching cannot be found by a simple reading of Scripture. The revealed Word of God is read and interpreted by the magisterium, under the permanent guidance of the Holy Spirit.

So, women cannot be ordained to the priesthood. Much further study will bring greater light on the subject, but the Church has spoken and we are not free, as Catholics, to reject the authoritative teaching of the magisterium. It is a dangerous and frightening thing to note how many American Catholics think they are free to dispute the teaching Church. As the German bishops said of dissenters, "...the arrogant and over-weening will one day have to render an account before God."

The 1976 decision of the Holy See did not treat the diaconate for women. It seems clear that there have been deaconesses in the past. Did they receive true sacramental ordination or was their status non-sacramental? This question is now being studied and will doubtless be clarified in time. I cannot offer a definitive solution.

(November, 1977)

THE FAITH OF YOUR CHILDREN—REGARDING DOCTRINE AND LIFE

Dear Father,

If we want our children to be taught the Faith, why don't we go back to the Baltimore Catechism?

Not-so-old

Dear Not-so-old,

The first edition of the Baltimore Catechism was published in 1885, to be followed by many other editions. Generations of Catholics in this country were solidly grounded in the Faith by this splendid little book, under, by and large, good teachers who fleshed out the bare bones of the questions and answers. Understandably, those who were raised on this catechism look upon it as a perduring, almost eternal compendium of the Faith.

But times change. The language, customs, attitudes and background of new generations differ, and we have to speak to people (including little people) in a vernacular they will understand. In addition, while the substance of the Faith does not change, our understanding of it can and does deepen, and it is a happy fact that in recent times we have learned a good deal about better methods of teaching.

Most of all, perhaps, our times have seen great advances in our appreciation of Sacred Scripture and the liturgy. The old Baltimore Catechism never envisioned the Mass in English, revised sacramental rites, not to mention the great new horizons of Vatican II. To put it briefly, the Church in our day is struggling to present to its people a richer and deeper view of the unchanging old Faith. This demands, inevitably, new catechetical approaches. It is not a question of a "new" Catholicism, but rather of a new and suitably up-to-date way of teaching the old Faith.

Not all the catechisms introduced in recent years have been satisfactory. The much publicized Dutch Catechism, for example, required emendation from Rome. Some of the catechisms produced in the United States have been criticized, even severely. It will take time to sort the chaff from the wheat, but it will be done. Meanwhile, parents, who are the first catechists (most of all by their good example), should check what their children are being taught, both as regards doctrine and the living of the Faith. Do they know their prayers and the Commandments? Do they reverence the Blessed Sacrament? Do they go to confession regularly? And so on....

If you have any notable reservations about what your children are taught, speak up, and in the meanwhile, try hard to supplement any deficiencies you may observe. Ask yourself if the youngsters have, for their age, a good grasp of (1) doctrine, and (2) the living of that doctrine. Answers memorized from a catechism, while good and even necessary, are not enough. The child who knows those answers must also be gently taught to weave them into real life as a prayerful, loving child of God.

(January, 1978)

WHAT DOES IT MEAN FOR A CATHOLIC TO BE "BORN AGAIN" IN THE SPIRIT?

Dear Father,
I have been a baptized Catholic all my life and tried my best to practice my Faith as best I could. Now a friend of mine, who was Catholic but is now, as she says, "Born Again," says I won't be saved unless I'm born again—quoting St. John's Gospel to back up her point. Can you please explain the truth to me more clearly?
A baptized Catholic

Dear Baptized Catholic,
Our Lord told Nicodemus (Jn. 3) that to enter the kingdom of God one must "be born again of water and the Spirit." The reference is to the Christian sacrament of Baptism. Classical Pentecostalism (Protestant), although it

recognizes Baptism, holds that the fullness of the Spirit comes with "Baptism in (or of) the Spirit."

There is only one Baptism (cf. Eph. 4:5). The term "Baptism in the Spirit" does not occur in the New Testament. There is no text to support the thesis that the coming of the Spirit is held back until a special "second blessing." Peter's Pentecost sermon ends with a request for conversion, baptism and reception of the gift of the Spirit. There is no hint that the Spirit is to come later; the *three elements* of initiation are all one.

Hence, your friend is wrong in saying that, in addition to the sacraments of initiation, you need another rebirth in order to be saved. Your one and only true rebirth took place at Baptism, when the new life of the resurrected Christ was given and the Spirit was communicated.

Catholic charismatics also use the term "Baptism in (or of) the Holy Spirit," but since there is no warrant in Scripture or Tradition for the Pentecostalist use of the term, Catholic charismatics mean, not a new sacrament, but the personally experienced actualization of grace already sacramentally received. So, for the Catholic charismatic there is a sound and altogether different understanding of the term. It is a moving spiritual experience. For the early Church, the Holy Spirit was an experience, but over the years there was a decline in this experiential dimension, which we might well rediscover.

Thus, there is no problem at all for baptized (and confirmed) Catholic Christians experiencing the Spirit in, say, the context of prayer, or in confession. Then, it can be said, a gift long ago received in Baptism may be reawakened with great impact, like the "second conversion" experience the saints and mystics speak of. Nonetheless, we are not trying to set up an elite group. Faith is always faith in what is not seen, and God is more than just our felt experience of Him. Catholic tradition approves of sound spiritual experiences. The Spirit is one, but His works are many. Some spiritual experiences are dramatic, some quiet and serene.

Your friend did not have to leave the Catholic Church to be "born again." She received that new birth at Baptism, and all subsequent experiences of the Spirit, however wonderful, were rooted in Baptism. May she return to the household of the Faith, where the Spirit will welcome her. There is one Lord, one Faith, one Baptism. We do not need to seek the Spirit, and may not, in far pastures. The good there is in the "born again" idea, properly understood, can be found in the Church, where the Spirit breathes as He wills. Whether He gives us soul-shaking experiences or simpler graces, may His will be done.

(March, 1979)

MORALS

"I CANNOT UNDERSTAND HER!"

Dear Father,

I hope you can give me some advice. I know this is not a new problem, but now that I'm faced with it myself I'm not sure what to do.

For almost nine months now my daughter has been living with a young man and they have no plans for marriage until he is out of the service.

Since the time she first told me she shared her apartment with him, I have refused to have anything to do with the boy—I don't even know what he looks like. I did this so that she could not say my attitude was caused by a personal dislike for him. I have made it clear that I am opposed to the immorality of their actions.

Our home is open to my daughter, and she does come frequently. She often says, however, "If only you'd meet him, you'd see how nice he is and that we are not doing anything wrong." They are asking to be accepted into the family as a couple. I cannot understand how a girl

If you think it might help, you may allow the young man into your home also, or you may follow your present course of refusing to see him. I suspect (but only you can judge this) that your other children might not suffer serious harm.

How did your daughter get this way, you wonder? She is a child of Adam and Eve, and self-deception is as old as our first parents. May you, her good mother, assist her back to the world of reality and the true love of God, of herself, and of her young man.

One last thing. Keep in mind another mother whose child lived in concubinage and almost broke her heart. But she prayed him back to God. Her name was St. Monica and he became St. Augustine.

(March, 1974)

THEY CAN'T UNDERSTAND...

Dear Father,

I never thought I'd be writing for advice. But, here I am and it came about this way.

At Sunday Mass I picked up the March copy of The Family, *the first issue of this magazine I'd ever seen.*

I read the first article, then turned to the second one, the "Letter of the Month"! I noted where readers were invited to write about prob-

lems and before I ever read the "Letter of the Month" and your answer, I resolved to write to you for help.

It is uncanny how this mother's problem and mine are so similar. It is almost like a "sign" I've been praying for!

Our beautiful, talented daughter, very successful in her career, has been, for a year or more, living with a young man.

They have no intention of getting married. They like their life the way it is.

He moved into her apartment; he uses her car; she keeps house and makes the living for them! Of course, he won't change things! She's the one who'll have to "call the shots."

The sad part is they can't understand why the family won't accept them as a couple. This we cannot do, though we have tried to keep the door open for our daughter (as you advised "Worried Mother"). However, right now, her father (age 77) is seriously considering disinheriting her. Should he do this? He cannot bear to think of contributing to and thereby condoning their way of life.

Having been educated in Catholic schools, through college, it is hard to understand how her values have become so distorted.

Do you have any additional advice for us, other than what you gave "Worried Mother"? What about cutting this daughter out of our wills?

Thank you so much, Father. It has helped just to write to you!

Gratefully,
A brokenhearted mother

Dear Brokenhearted Mother,

I am very sorry to hear of the sorrow you have to bear from your daughter. This kind of thing, I must say, is more and more common and flows from a general social breakdown and, worst of all, a breakdown in the Catholicity of many.

In addition to what I said in the March "Letter of the Month," this is what I would suggest:

The thing we want to avoid is anything that will harden the heart of your daughter and give her an excuse to be bitter against you and, in consequence, the Church. So try hard to keep in touch with her without ever condoning her manner of life. Sooner or later, we may hope, she will get the message.

I would not, either, suggest that she be cut out of your wills. However, if you wish, it might be a salutary thing to leave a letter with the will, telling your daughter of the sorrow she has brought you and begging her to reconcile herself with God. So, when she gets the legacy, she also will get one she may not have anticipated, and it could well be very salutary.

This way, you will have done all that anyone could ask of good parents. You will have been patient, loving, forgiving, but never condoning.

Meanwhile, commend her to God every day. She has been with this man only a year (only!), and I would not be surprised that fairly soon she may begin to realize that she has been very foolish, sinful, and, actually, deceived.

You are in my Masses and prayers. May our Lord, who knows how, bring you every comfort.

(May, 1974)

FOLLOW MY FEELINGS?

Reverend Father,

My boss's son is a Brother (religious). A few weeks ago we were talking about Sunday Mass. I told him I did not go and he said, "If you feel that it is not a serious sin to miss Sunday Mass, then for you, it is not a sin."

I was glad he told me that then. However, now I am doubting it. If it is a serious sin to miss Mass, I am in trouble. Please help me. I do not want to commit serious sin.

Weak and Confused

Dear Weak and Confused,

Why does the Church require us to observe Sunday? Not just to be sure that the pews are full, but for only one reason: *because it is the Mass that matters.* As Vatican II put it:

> "...the liturgy is the summit toward which the activity of the Church is directed; at the same time it is the fountain from which all her power flows. For the goal of apostolic works is that all who are made sons of God by faith and baptism should come together to praise God in the midst of His Church, to take part in her sacrifice and to eat the Lord's Supper" (*Constitution on the Liturgy*, no. 10).

The Council obviously wants to teach us the absolute centrality of the Eucharist in Catholic life. Mass on Sunday is supposed to be the most important thing we do all week. When Vatican II speaks of the obligation to participate in this Mass, it says in one place that we "ought" to gather together, and in another that "the faithful are bound on Sundays and feast days to attend the divine liturgy...."

It should be clear that the highest teaching authority in the Church stresses our obligation to Sunday Mass. There is no hint that the standard, accepted teaching has been changed. Quite the contrary. I would suggest that no ecumenical Council in history ever stressed the centrality of the Mass so vigorously.

Nonetheless, in recent years, some Catholics have been saying—and on their own authority alone, mind you—that missing Sunday Mass now and then, even without a good reason, is not sinful. Their argument seems to be that God would not want to bind under pain of mortal sin in such a "trivial" (so to speak) matter.

I respond: (1) Sunday Mass attendance is not a trivial matter. It should be the high point of the week for every Catholic. (2) God said of His Church, "Who hears you hears me." And the Church, speaking in His name, tells us that Mass on Sundays and holydays is simply a must.

The Church could, of course, mitigate that obligation somewhat, but there is no evidence that she has done so, and until the Pope and the bishops do make a change (quite unlikely) the obligation remains a serious one.

I assume that we all realize that there are excuses which allow us to miss Mass without sin—sickness, other obligations, etc. Also, your pastor can give you a dispensation.

The fundamental reason why some Catholics find Sunday Mass a burden is that they do not grasp, even vaguely, the tremendous meaning of the Eucharist. To put it simply, the Mass is the most important thing happening anywhere on earth at any given time. For at Mass we celebrate our Lord's death and resurrection, the divine act which overcame sin and death, reconciled us sinners to God and showed us perfect love in its most perfect form. Sunday, the first day of the week, recalls the creation of the world and the resur-

rection. It is the Day of the Lord. On this one
day of the week, at least, we must give
ourselves especially to God.

If we grasp these ideas even imperfectly,
there would be no need for a law to oblige us to
Mass. We would run to church, eagerly, glad-
ly. But because we are weak and forgetful,
Holy Mother Church reminds us of our duty.

So your boss's son gave you bad advice
about the obligation of Sunday Mass and also
confused advice about following your conscience. It is not our subjective view that makes
right or wrong. We are bound to follow the
truth, as far as we know it, and not our own
feelings or preferences.

I am sure you will start going to Mass
again with, I hope, a deeper appreciation of
the Church's wisdom.

(July-August, 1975)

DO WE TAKE THEM IN?

Dear Father,

*I often hear parents wondering what at-
titudes they should take concerning daughters
or sons who are living common-law. Should
they visit them and invite them into their
homes?*

*If it would happen to me (I'm a mother of
three), I'd invite my child, but not his "wife."
Suppose they'd have children? I guess I'd be
more lenient. If we received them in our home*

*and they kept on living together, couldn't this
be a proof to them that we approve of their
"shacking up"?*

*I'd like a clear answer on this question as
so many parents are involved with this problem.*

I thank you in advance.

Interested

Dear Interested,

First, there is no answer that will fit every
situation perfectly. In a sense, you have to
"play it by ear" to a certain extent. But in
general, something like the following would be
good advice:

First, tell your son very clearly that he is
living in sin and that neither you, the Church,
nor God can approve. This is not just legalism.
Marriage is a holy sacrament for life, and not
just a casual living together. Neither does
"love," however real and true, make holy what
is not holy.

It will not be wise to express your disapproval too often. Don't harp on it. Just be sure
they know what you think and that you mean it.

The main idea from now on is to keep the
friendship of the pair in the hope that someday
they will see the error of their ways and remedy
things. Experience seems to teach that when
parents reject and cast out their sinful children
in situations like this, the offspring may well
react bitterly by rejecting God and His Church.
Nobody wins that way.

We have to love sinners, all of them. We do not condone their sin, but we try, gently and patiently, to bring them back to their senses and God.

So, if the children and your neighbors (if necessary) know of your clear disapproval of this bad common-law marriage, then you may in clear conscience have the pair, and any children they have, in to see you.

Meanwhile, never stop praying for them.

(September, 1975)

"ARE WE MORALLY BOUND TO STAY ALIVE?"

Dear Father,

I'm all confused about the "right-to-die" theory that I see publicized here and there. In what way is this related to euthanasia? Back in my college days I think I remember studying that while a person must take normal measures to save his health he is not morally bound to use extraordinary means to stay alive. Could you please clarify all these points?

Gratefully,
A worried inquirer

Dear Worried Inquirer,

Euthanasia, often called mercy killing, refers to the painless killing of a person whose life is a burden because of incurable illness, old age, handicaps, etc. The word euthanasia means happy death, but, to call a spade a spade, it is actually either murder or suicide. Vatican II in *The Church in the Modern World*, no. 27, calls it an "infamy."

Many Americans believe in and promote euthanasia. Some have taken to calling it "the right to die," as if man had complete rights over himself even to the point of deciding the hour of his death. The fact is that man's most fundamental human right is the right to *live*, and man cannot renounce that right. Anyone who takes his own life or the life of another out of misplaced pity is playing God, for only God, the giver of life, has supreme dominion over it.

Euthanasia is, then, intrinsically evil because it entails a direct violation of man's most fundamental and inalienable right, the right to life. It is forbidden by the natural law, divine positive law and human positive law. "You shall not kill."

Those who defend euthanasia have lost any sense of the Christian concept of suffering. We want, certainly, to eliminate as much pain and suffering as we can, but when we have done all in our power, we bow our heads before God's mysterious providence and, in faith, try to make suffering a means of purification, penance and sanctification. Christ in Gethsemane did not call to be put out of His pain, but spoke words that have been the comfort of broken hearts down the centuries: "My Fa-

ther, if it is possible, let this cup pass me by.
Still, let it be as you would have it, not as I"
(Mt. 26:39).

A special problem today, quite different
from euthanasia, is the capacity of modern
medicine to keep people alive. Normally, one is
held to use only ordinary means to preserve his
life. It is important to keep in mind that doctors
and theologians have different things in mind
when they speak of "ordinary" or "extraordinary" means. "Ordinary" for the doctor
means standard, established, current, medical
practice. "Extraordinary" would refer to the
experimental or the rare. Theologically, however, an ordinary means to preserve life would
be one that gives reasonable hope of benefit,
is available without excessive expense, pain
or other similar complications. Extraordinary
means would be treatment demanding excessive costs, pain, etc., or which might not offer
reasonable hope of benefit. If a patient is
already virtually dead, there is no obligation to
use artificial means to support life. We can stop
using them with clear conscience and, as Pope
Pius XII said in 1957, "...allow the patient...to
depart in peace."

Since it can be quite unsettling to be faced
with unexpected decisions about ordinary and
extraordinary means for prolonging life, some
people are making a "living will" in order
to spare their relatives and doctors unnecessary

anguish. I append the text as prepared by the Catholic Hospital Association, St. Louis, Missouri, 63104.

Christian Affirmation
of Life

As a result of a desire to avoid unnecessary suffering and expense at the time of terminal illness, many people wish to sign a "living will." The Christian Affirmation of Life is designed to meet the needs of Christians who wish to sign such a document. Expressing truths of the Christian faith that are concerned with all levels of life, it considers death as the last human act leading to eternal life. The Christian Affirmation of Life is a document of reflection and reference, rather than a legal document.

To my family, friends, physician, lawyer and clergyman:

I believe that each individual person is created by God our Father in love and that God retains a loving relationship to each person throughout human life and eternity.

I believe that Jesus Christ lived, suffered, and died for me and that His suffering, death, and resurrection prefigure and make possible the death-resurrection process which I now anticipate.

I believe that each person's worth and dignity derives from the relationship of love in Christ that God has for each individual person, and not from one's usefulness or effectiveness in society.

I believe that God our Father has entrusted to me a shared dominion with Him over my earthly existence so that I am bound to use ordinary means to preserve my life, but I am free to refuse extraordinary means to prolong my life.

I believe that through death, life is not taken away but merely changed, and though I may experience fear, suffering, and sorrow, by the grace of the Holy Spirit, I hope to accept death as a free human act which enables me to surrender this life and to be united with God for eternity.

Because of my belief:

I, _____, request that I be informed as death approaches so that I may continue to prepare for the full encounter with Christ through the help of the sacraments and the consolation and prayers of my family and friends.

I request that, if possible, I be consulted concerning the medical procedures which might be used to prolong my life as death approaches. If I can no longer take part in decisions concerning my own future and there is no reasonable expectation of my recovery from

physical and mental disability, I request that
no extraordinary means be used to prolong
my life.

I request, though I wish to join my suffering to the suffering of Jesus so I may be united
fully with Him in the act of death-resurrection,
that my' pain, if unbearable, be alleviated.
However, no means should be used with the intention of shortening my life.

I request, because I am a sinner and in
need of reconciliation and because my faith,
hope, and love may not overcome all fear and
doubt, that my family, friends, and the whole
Christian community join me in prayer and
mortification as I prepare for the great personal
act of dying.

Finally, I request that after my death, my
family, my friends, and the whole Christian
community pray for me, and rejoice with me
because of the mercy and love of the Trinity,
with whom I hope to be united for all eternity.

Signed _____

Date_____

(October, 1975)

...PRODIGAL

Dear Father,

I have a long-standing habit of masturbation. When it started, I did not know it was a
serious sin, and anyway, I was not much of a

Catholic. Now I'm trying to straighten out my life before God, and I wonder if you could help me.

...Prodigal

Dear Prodigal,

If you did not know that masturbation was in itself seriously wrong, then, of course, you did not sin seriously. But now you know better. Before I give you any practical advice, let me fill in the general picture.

The Church has always taught that masturbation is objectively seriously wrong. The basic reason for this is that all deliberate use of sex must be exercised only in marriage. Our sexual faculties were not given to us by God merely for our private pleasure. They were given to us to be used in marriage, where husband and wife give themselves in love to each other in acts always open to the begetting of children. This does not mean that they must have a dozen or so babies, necessarily; but it does mean that their mutual self-giving does not deliberately hinder offspring in any forbidden way.

As you can see, the use of sex in masturbation is not directed at all towards either possible children or legitimate love of another. It is closed in on self.

It is, then, objectively wrong. But in addition to an objectively evil act, there must also be sufficient reflection and full consent of the will to constitute a subjectively serious sin. Quite a number of things can hinder the required reflection and consent. If a person does not know that masturbation is wrong, he does not, obviously, consent to any wrong. Immaturity in the adolescent, and even among some older people, can diminish the deliberate character of the act so that subjectively the fault may not be serious. The same holds for ingrained habit, which is so hard to eradicate. In addition, we arc all weak as a result of original sin, and our weakness is not helped by the erotic climate in which we live.

So, then, in summary: masturbation in itself is gravely forbidden, but the judgment of serious fault in any individual case must be quite personal. There can be, often enough, reasons to indicate that culpability was not grave.

Those who habitually try to keep God's law in every way they can are less likely to sin seriously. It is up to the individual to find out and use the natural and supernatural means to overcome this problem.

My best advice to you is to see a priest, in or out of confession, and get advice tailored to your situation. Rooting out an old habit is tough work. Go to confession regularly, pray hard, and do not for a moment give in to discouragement. God, you know, is our loving Father, not an ogre. He loves you as if you were the only person in the world—God can manage that! Patience, and courage.

(October, 1976)

THE LORD'S GREAT GIFT

Dear Father,
My 16-year-old daughter hasn't gone to confession for three years. She says a good Act of Contrition is enough to make up for her sins. "After all, confession is only for mortal sin." How should I answer her?

A concerned mother

Dear Concerned Mother,
Your daughter is the unwitting victim of a very strange malaise which has spread through parts of the Church. I mean the abandonment, or near abandonment, of frequent confession. Good Catholics, in the very recent past, went to confession often. Now, despite the fact that Communion lines are long, few seem to keep up the practice of confessions of "devotion," i.e., confession of venial sins only. I cannot wholly understand this unfortunate development, but I am sure that one feature of it is a loss of the sense of the malice of sin, including venial sin, not to mention the precious value inherent in the reception of a sacrament.

The Holy See is aware of the situation. In June, 1972, the Sacred Congregation for the Doctrine of the Faith urged priests to recommend the "rich benefits for Christian living" of frequent or devotional confessions. The Congregation warned priests not to dare to dissuade the faithful from such confessions, and in a section which concerns your daughter and others who think as she does, wrote: "What must be altogether avoided is that individual confession be reserved for mortal sins alone; such a practice would deprive the faithful of the best benefit of confession and would harm the reputation of those who individually approach the sacrament."

A more recent Roman decree of December, 1973, establishing the new Order of Penance, earnestly recommends frequent confession of venial sins alone.

It is not sound Catholic doctrine, therefore, to say that confession is "only for mortal sin." It is true that one is not bound under pain of sin to go to confession when one has no mortal sins, but the sacrament is not reserved exclusively for grave sinners. It is for all sinners, and most of the sins of us sinners are venial. They are, nonetheless, real sins, offenses against God and His Church, for which we have need of reconciliation. If we do not confess our venial sins, we will still be in God's grace, but we will lose more than a great deal. Frequent confession of venial sins brings us, first of all, an increase in grace, surely no small gift from God. In addition, we grow in knowledge of our own weakness; we grow in humility; we may receive much-needed advice to take the blinkers off our selfish eyes.

One particular benefit, in my opinion, is that frequent confession brings a greater appreciation of the Holy Eucharist. Without a knowledge of our own sinfulness (from venial sins, large or small), we are likely to approach Mass and Holy Communion in a routine, casual fashion. I may be wrong, but I am afraid that this kind of approach is too common today.

In normal, good, Catholic life, frequent confessions of devotion should be a standard feature. Practically and pastorally speaking, I would fear very much for the perseverance of Catholics who rarely go to confession. They are like people on a poor diet who wonder why their health is deteriorating.

Many of you readers may well have slipped from your former practice of frequent confession. I would urge you, both for your own good and as an apostolate of good example, to return to frequent confession. We all have a deep need of our Lord's great gift of the sacrament of Reconciliation. The current fashion of confessing rarely is pernicious, and should be stopped.

(November, 1976)

THE AUTHENTIC TEACHING

Dear Father,

One hears much today about tubal tying which we believe to be seriously wrong. Is it permissible to tie tubes to prevent pregnancy because another pregnancy would mean the

death of the mother? We can understand where
cancerous tubes would have to be removed and
the indirect result would be an impossibility to
become pregnant; but to tie tubes in order that
one cannot become pregnant seems seriously
wrong.

Sincerely,
An inquirer

Dear Inquirer,

Your question is timely, since some Catholics in this country have been saying that direct sterilization, which is done precisely to prevent pregnancy, is permissible. Ligation (or tying) of the fallopian tubes is a common surgical means to induce contraceptive infertility. It is forbidden. The Ethical and Religious Directives for Catholic Health Facilities issued by the United States Catholic Conference in 1971, state (no. 18): "Sterilization, whether permanent or temporary, for men or for women, may not be used as a means of contraception."

This clear teaching of the American bishops was disputed by some theologians, so, in March, 1975, the Holy See firmly reiterated Catholic teaching in reply of the Congregation for the Doctrine of the Faith to questions submitted by the bishops of the United States. Here is part of Rome's reply:

"Any sterilization which of itself, that is, of its own nature and condition, has the sole immediate effect of rendering the generative faculty incapable of procreation, is to be considered direct sterilization, as the term is understood in the declarations of the Pontifical Magisterium, especially of Pius XII. Therefore, notwithstanding any subjectively right intention of those whose actions are prompted by the care or prevention of physical or mental illness which is foreseen or feared as a result of pregnancy, such sterilization remains absolutely forbidden according to the doctrine of the Church...."

The Congregation goes on to state that it is aware that some theologians differ with this teaching. The views of these dissenters, says the Congregation firmly, cannot be accepted or followed.

Hence, tying the tubes for directly contraceptive purposes, even if a consequence may be therapeutic, is wrong. The real aim is contraception. If another pregnancy would really mean the death of the mother, then pregnancy should be avoided by moral means, not by the immoral one of direct sterilization.

If tubes are cancerous, they may be tied, even if the indirect result would be sterilization. The therapeutic goal here is not sterilization immediately, but the care of the cancer. Sterilization is not directly intended, but only permitted.

The lesson here: the authentic teachers of morals are the bishops in union with the Pope. Dissenting theologians may not be followed.

(June, 1977)

WHAT ABOUT MORTAL SIN?

Dear Father,

Please explain the Church's teaching on sin, especially serious sin. I have recently heard of the term "the fundamental option." What does this mean? It seems to eliminate what used to be called "mortal sin."

A confused penitent

Dear Confused Penitent,

The term "fundamental option" can be used to refer to a person's basic moral disposition. If my deep-down and permanent attitude is one of wanting to love and serve God, and never to offend Him seriously, then my fundamental option is sound and good. If, on the contrary, I am one who habitually loves self more than God and does not really worry much about offending Him, even in grave matters, then my fundamental option is a choice of evil.

This acceptable meaning of the term can be abused. Some talk as if it would be almost impossible for a basically good man (one whose usual moral disposition is to follow God's law) to fall into mortal sin. They seem to say that if a basically good man does something gravely sinful, then it is not gravely sinful for him. One act, they hold, is not enough to separate him from God; a series of gravely forbidden acts is required. It is almost as if one had to shake his fist at God, contemptuously, to commit a grave sin.

This is not the teaching of the Church. Just because a man is basically good, it cannot be said that his bad acts are good. It is true that we have learned much in recent years about subjective attitudes which can reduce culpability. But man today is just as free as he always was. He is still quite able to choose good or evil. And he can do it in a single act which turns him aside from his normal path of goodness, most of all when he has carelessly (but freely) weakened his moral fiber by a number of deliberate venial sins.

The traditional, approved teaching of the Church certainly takes into account the sinner's subjective intention and involvement. But it also reminds us that some things are seriously commanded or forbidden. There are acts we must perform and acts we must avoid. It cannot be said that only a monster is capable of mortal sin. We might just as well say that only an angel—not a mere man—is capable of permanent virtuous living.

It might be possible to say that the fundamental option is only a new way of looking at the depth and seriousness of choice involved in moral judgments, with due recognition of the matter and reflection involved. Unhappily, a good deal of the speculation, at this point, departs from Catholic teaching. Extreme proponents of the fundamental option all but eliminate mortal sin from human experience.

We do not lightly fall into mortal sin. But we *can* sin mortally. We do so when we freely and consciously choose something which is seriously disordered. We are not robots. We are free, able to opt for good or evil.

I strongly suspect that false ideas about this whole matter are behind the current drop-off in confessions. People are beginning to act as if mortal sin is just not something that could enter their lives. So they go to confession rarely or never.

As always, follow the Pope and the bishops who teach in communion with him. Ignore teachers who talk as if mortal sin were out-of-date. Our Lord did not die to redeem the sinless, nor did He suffer only to atone for peccadillos. I am not saying that the average good Catholic's life is shot through with terrible sins. I am only saying what the Church says: that mortal sin is always an awesome possibility for all of us.

(May, 1978)

MOVIE-GOERS AND MORAL NORMS

Reverend Father,
The other night, our teenage daughter casually mentioned that she didn't understand why she couldn't go to "R" rated movies.

She goes to Catholic school and has always been an obedient child, so this kind of shocked us, and none of our answers satisfied her. Could you please help us, Father?
                                        Concerned Parents

Dear Concerned Parents,

The "R" rating of the Motion Picture Association of America (not a sound moral guide) means that those under seventeen will not be admitted without a parent or adult guardian. It is an implicit admission that films of this type are unsuitable for these teenagers unless responsible (or perhaps irresponsible) adults judge otherwise. Catholics should follow the ratings of the National Catholic Office for Motion Pictures, which are far more reliable. They can be found in Catholic diocesan newspapers and, rather often, in the vestibules of churches.

Why these ratings? Simply because the movies are a tremendous force for good or evil. Not everyone, least of all a teenager, has the kind of discriminating taste necessary to evaluate the flood of films. The National Catholic Office for Motion Pictures (successor to the Legion of Decency) aims at forming moral and aesthetic sensitivity by means of its ratings. Their judgments are made after thirty, forty or more professional reviewers evaluate the film. We should be grateful that they can save us from what is, artistically, trash, or, morally, the possible occasion of sin.

The Holy See has long been aware of the cultural value and the moral danger of movies. From the time of Pius X to Vatican II, the Holy See has issued some 130 documents on movies, two of them major encyclicals. It is not at all a matter of narrow-minded censorship. The Church wants to encourage good movies because of their great cultural value, and at the same time she insists that movie-goers need moral norms and an awareness of personal responsibility. Some movies are unfit for some people, particularly youngsters, and some are unfit for all.

So, the reason why there are ratings which restrict your teenager is simply the fact that some movies would do her moral and/or cultural harm. We are all children of Adam and Eve, open to temptation and sin. We need to learn from the wisdom of experience. We have had, in the United States, a great deal of experience, much of it bitter, in the last fifty years of movies. The film industry needs regulation, primarily the regulation of informed patrons who flatly refuse to patronize junk or immorality.

Given the special impact of movies on moral and cultural values, any system of ratings which improves the quality of films is a blessing for individuals and society at large. Our Catholic ratings are not over strict; rather, the offerings they evaluate are often appalling.

By refusing our patronage to bad movies, we are being good Catholics and good citizens.

(April, 1979)

A DANGEROUS GAME

Dear Father,

For some time now my sister (who is a Catholic) has been putting a lot of stock in the Ouija board. How can I best explain to her that this practice is really not allowed by our Faith? At first she began by only using it as a game, but now she's gotten serious about it.

Someone Desiring To Help

Dear Someone Desiring To Help

The use of the Ouija board can be just a game. If the players mean no harm and if the answers can be explained naturally (v.g., as coming from conscious or subconscious knowledge, a good guess, etc.), there is no sin. Some of the things the board "tells" us may be due to the operation of our subconscious mind, a reservoir of forgotten past feelings and experiences.

However, if we eliminate answers which stem from natural causes, good guesses, coincidence, fraud and, possibly, natural powers we do not yet understand, what other sources can we look to? We are not appealing to nature, reason or God. Hence, most likely, the implied source of knowledge is the devil. I feel quite sure that most people would not admit this and would not intend it. But the possibility is there and logic points in that frightening direction.

Thus, we can be talking of the sin of divination, which seeks to learn hidden events, particularly future hidden events, by either express or tacit appeal to the devil for aid. Only God knows the acts a person is to perform freely and deliberately in the future. The devil can only guess, but we are equivalently attributing to him a power which belongs to God alone.

I can sin by use of the Ouija board when I seek answers about the secret past of others, about free future acts known only to God, or when the answers are expected to come from the dead or demons.

Sometimes, even when people are playing the game more or less innocently, the answers may purport to reveal the secret thoughts of the participants. Good and guiltless people can be deeply hurt, to the embarrassment, and perhaps the suspicion, of others present.

It should be fairly clear that the Ouija board can be a very dangerous game. I am not saying that mature and sensible players will necessarily go astray, but the peril is there. Some types are particularly susceptible to the occult. There is a morbid fascination which can turn a game into a dark obsession. There are plenty of harmless diversions. This one can be very harmful. The only sensible course is to discourage the use of the Ouija board, even when it seems just a simple pastime. Your sister, obviously, needs to throw away her board and forget it.

(May, 1979)

BIBLE

"IT WAS A LONG WAY
TO THE PURE MORALITY..."

Dear Father,
If God said, "You shall not kill," why did
the Israelites kill the Canaanites?
A puzzled student

Dear Puzzled Student,

The Fifth Commandment forbids murder, which is the direct and unlawful killing of another person. Taking another's life can be justified, however, in proper self-defense, which is the case in a just war.

The Israelites certainly considered their war against the Canaanites just. In fact, they considered it a "holy war." If we are to understand what took place at Jericho, for example, we must try to grasp the attitude of the Israelites. God had promised His Chosen People the Promised Land. The wars mentioned in the Book of Joshua were wars of conquest to take over that land. Those were primitive times, and the people had primitive notions. War is always harsh and brutal, especially a war of annihilation. Nonetheless, the Israelites in all simplicity thought that by killing all the Canaanites they were performing a holy act.

They considered the destruction of everything in Jericho as a way to dedicate all of it to Yahweh, to eliminate the possibility of enriching themselves by booty, and simultaneously to protect themselves and their religion from contamination.

The Bible is not giving us precise, detailed historical records of what happened. There is real historical foundation in what is said, but the essential message is that God had promised them this land and He kept His promise. To describe God's fidelity to His promise, they assumed that God led them, protected them, and approved of what they did in detail. So they acted according to their primitive lights, and their actions cannot all be justified objectively.

How can we explain this? By remembering that God made His will known to men in stages. He tolerated some things and corrected them later by more complete revelation. Much of what was done in the conquest of the Promised Land is indefensible in the light of our Christian morality. But the Israelites were not Christians. They must be accepted for what they were. We cannot judge them by our standards. It was a long way to the pure morality taught by our Lord.

For those who might be scandalized by the killing of the Canaanites, I would suggest a little reflection on modern war, with its atomic bomb, and the obliteration bombing of whole cities. Not to mention the incredible cruelty of abortion, legalized in our own country.

God was patient with the crudities of His Chosen People. Somehow He is patient with us, when we know better, or should.

So, the story of Israel's advance into the Promised Land, harsh and primitive though it may be in parts, is not a canonization of sin or cruelty, but is, essentially, a record of God's faithful keeping of His Word. In time, the crude ways of the past would be purified. We can never accuse God of the errors and ignorance of all His people. He is a God of love, as He showed so splendidly when, in time, He sent us His Son.   (January, 1979)

MYTH OR TRUTH?

Dear Father,

Just now that I have come to love the Bible, though not always understanding the Old Testament, I have been told at a recent Bible study that much of the Old Testament is based on myth.

Where is myth and where is truth? Who draws the line...? Kindly explain.

Perplexed

Dear Perplexed,

Communication is a tricky business. If words are not used properly, or if they are not explained carefully, they can cause trouble. That's why lawyers make a good living!

The word "myth" as applied to the Bible is one of those very tricky words that require explanation. Let me try, briefly....

Myth in ordinary modern usage usually means something that is pure fiction, a lie, an old wives' tale. In this sense of the word, there are absolutely no myths in the Bible.

There is, however, another use of the word. In this sense a "myth" is a literary form (just as a novel or a poem is a literary form) which is used to try to express supernatural, transcendent truth in a dramatic way.

I can, for example, talk about creation in abstract philosophical terms or in complex theological concepts. The book of Genesis tells us the story of creation through the literary form of myth. The writers of Genesis did not have the historical information or the scientific data necessary to write a treatise on creation, so they expressed the basic truths of the matter in myth.

Note that they expressed the *truths* involved. Myths are used by the Bible not just as stories or fables like the pagan myths of the same period from which the inspired writers borrowed some elements. The decisive events are in a real sense historical, for they reveal God's activity in our midst.

Perhaps the chief point that must be made clear is that the ancients had no notion of scientific history as we think of it today. But they knew that the narratives in the Bible tell the essential truths involved. And, of course, since the writers of the Bible were inspired, the accuracy of their message is divinely guaranteed. And the divine guarantee is made for the Bible as written, i.e., in this case God guarantees myth, properly understood, as a vehicle for revealed truth.

It is quite an exaggeration to say that "much of the Old Testament is based on myth." A very great deal of it isn't. Scripture scholars are the ones, under the guidance of the Church, who dig out the details for us. They deserve our prayers for a very hard but rewarding work.

I hope you can now see that we don't have to "draw a line" between myth and truth. There are no lying myths in the Bible, only myths (properly understood) which tell us truths often too profound for scientific observation or philosophical analysis. They are truths God wants us to know—and He gave them to us in a form strange to us moderns, but quite sensible once it is explained.

(July-August, 1974)

"I'M CONFUSED ABOUT THE BIBLE"

Dear Father,
I've had something on my mind that I would like cleared up. Some people have been

coming to my house rather regularly to discuss the Bible. They confront me with Bible quotes. Now, I've always wanted to know more about the Bible, but they confuse me.

For instance, they show me passages about not adoring images—of wood, stone, precious metals. I told them that we do not adore images, but they keep coming back to those quotes in the Bible. I know that these people take the Scriptures very literally. Yet we, too, base our Faith on the Bible.

How is this problem about images answered, and what basic idea should I keep in mind about literal reading of Scriptures?

Respectfully,
Eager To Know

Dear Friend,

We Catholics base our Faith on the Bible, but only on the Bible interpreted authentically by Tradition and the Magisterium, i.e., the Pope and the bishops or the Pope alone. God did not give us the Bible and say, as it were, "Make what you can out of it." No. He gave us a book, the Bible, but He also gave us a Church to tell us what it means.

The Church, guided always by the Holy Spirit, has told us on more than one occasion that, while God alone is to be worshiped, veneration may be paid to images, not because they have any special worth of their own, but because of the person they represent. We do not give to creatures the worship due to God; that is idolatry.

Your Bible visitors seem unable to sort out the meaning of the many statements in Scripture, starting with the first commandment, which forbids idolatry. The Old Testament prohibition of images was intended to impress upon the people that God was immensely beyond anything that man could see or picture, and that He alone was to be adored. But none of the texts in either the Old or the New Testament can be applied to any and all veneration of images. Idolatry and veneration are quite simply two different things. From the earliest days the Church has venerated images and relics as reminders of saints who can teach us how to love God beyond all else.

The texts about images, then, are not hard to handle. They are not a problem among Christians of any kind except the most literal-minded. Still, the confusion about them among such people does show (1) the need for scholarship in reading the Bible, and (2) the absolute necessity of a teaching authority to tell us what Scripture means.

As Vatican II says in the *Constitution on Divine Revelation*, no. 10, "The task of authentically interpreting the word of God, whether written or handed on, has been entrusted exclusively to the living teaching authority of the

Church, whose authority is exercised in the name of Jesus Christ."

When you and I read Scripture, there are some things we should keep in mind: they were written long ago, in other languages, amid quite different cultural patterns. To cope with writings of that sort demands great scholarship. But after the scholars have told us all they can about the text, it may still, here and there, be open to various, quite different interpretations. Only the authentic Tradition of the Church and the teaching of the Magisterium can tell us what the inspired author intended to say.

I would suggest that you get some Catholic works of the Bible for your own reading. The Daughters of St. Paul have quite a number available in their Centers (the addresses are at the end of this book—and they did not ask me to put in this plug!). I think you should tell your Bible visitors, courteously but firmly, that hereafter you will do your Bible studies yourself. I do not doubt the sincerity of these good people, but they are not reliable teachers of the Bible.

(April, 1975)

READING THE BIBLE WITH PROFIT

Dear Father:

Where did Adam and Eve's children get their wives? How could the waters of the Red

Sea part? It seems to me that the Church has different answers for these questions, depending on whether children or adults are addressed.

A disillusioned teenager

Dear Disillusioned Teenager,

I am not quite sure what you mean when you say that the Church has "different" answers for children and adults. Be that as it may, it is a basic principle in education that knowledge must be imparted in a manner which suits the learners. A teacup cannot hold what a gallon jug will. A child cannot grasp what an adult can. An uneducated person cannot follow the reasoning and explanations of a university professor.

Sacred Scripture is learned the way anything is learned. A child will read the account of Creation and will take it for granted that every last detail of the story is a literal description of what happened. He will read the Exodus description of the crossing of the Red Sea in the same way. But as he grows older, if he has the advantage of a good Catholic education, he will begin to realize that Scripture, like any book, must be read the way it was intended to be read. Many parts of the Bible were not intended to be strict, detailed history, but rather, in the fashion of ancient writing, a literary description of religious truth. The essential idea to be conveyed was dressed in poetic images mixed with sober fact. Does this mean that the inspired authors are lying to us? Not at all. They are merely writing in the manner which was customary in their time, a fashion of writing which is not familiar to us moderns and which has to be painfully learned by scholars. And, keep in mind, this (to us) strange manner of writing is the one God chose to use to impart to us His teaching. This is not to say that all the Bible is poetic and obscure, clear only to specialists. It is only to say that *some* parts of the Bible require scholarly explanations, under the guidance of the Church, for us to arrive at the meaning intended by the inspired writer and God who inspired them.

Now to your questions. The story of creation says nothing about the wives of Adam and Eve's children. All that we can say with certitude is that somehow God arranged matters. The narrative of creation was not intended to be a straight history of what actually happened. The author of Genesis was not a witness of the event, after all. But what he taught, and what is revealed, is something beyond science and historical investigation. He is telling us that God created the universe and man, and many other fundamental truths.

Similarly, the story of the crossing of the Red Sea is concerned with the historical fact of Israel's deliverance, but the story is told with literary embellishments. The towering walls of water were most likely not so tall, but still enough to be a striking sign of God's providence.

To read the Bible with profit, we need help, at least in some instances. This means that what the naïve eyes of a child see in some passages will be somewhat different—and sometimes notably different—from what the mature and more learned will see. And, I may say, the more one learns about Sacred Scripture, the more one's heart burns with gratitude to the loving God who has so richly revealed Himself to us. It is not a matter of "stories for kids" and some sad, cynical reality for scholars. Quite the contrary. It is rather an unfolding of the riches of God's dealings with us, endlessly beautiful and consoling.

In sum, we do not have different and contradictory answers for different age groups. We have only the human necessity of taking in what we are able to grasp, given our experience, education, and so on. All of us should try to deepen our knowledge of the Bible. It isn't always easy, but it's worth the effort—very much so.

(February, 1978)

FAMILY

"MY MOTHER IS
LIVING WITH US..."

Dear Father,
Please, can you advise me on a difficult situation in our home that is growing more tense as time passes.

I am a mother of five children (ages 6 to 13). Several years ago my father passed away. Since that time my mother has been living with us—because we want her to and she enjoys being around the children.

The problem is that in the past few years she seems to be less able to care for herself, or to be left alone. Our financial situation is such that I have been seriously considering going out to work during school hours.

Both my husband and I agreed long ago that we would keep mother with us. I notice that recently my husband is getting more tense (and mother is more difficult to take care of), yet we cannot seem to talk it over. There is an uneasiness in our home that we never had before.

Yesterday one of my neighbors remarked pointedly that my first duty is to my family and

husband, yet I cannot stand the thought of tak-
ing any step that would make mother feel un-
wanted.

What is the right thing to do?

Gratefully,
Devoted Daughter, Wife and Mother

Dear Friend,

The first thing you should do is to try to talk this problem out with your husband. The neighbor's pointed remark seems to indicate that everybody is talking about it except you!

I suspect that your husband is torn between loyalty to you and growing inability to cope with your mother as she ages. He wants to keep his promise to care for her, but it's very hard. Maybe your inability to seek needed work during school hours has something to do with it. And so, tension and unhappiness.

I cannot be sure that I am reading your situation accurately, but that's what it seems to be. One thing is very clear: you must talk it over with your husband, frankly and honestly, to find out what's bothering him.

I do not know if you will find it possible to keep your mother at home without real danger to your marriage, once the air is cleared by discussion. If you and your husband can see your way to keeping her with you, even with the inevitable problems, then that is the best thing to do, and God will give you courage.

All the same, if you come to the conclusion, anguished though it be, that it is really a choice between your mother and your marriage, then I would urge you to find a place for her outside your home.

Neither solution will be easy, I know. Since the garden of Eden, God has never promised us a rose garden. Come to a decision as honestly and objectively as you can and then follow it in peace. May our Lord give you light.

(March, 1975)

"THEY'VE LOST THEIR MOTHER TOO…"

Dear Father,

My daughter has been married for fifteen years and has six children. Several months ago one of the boys (a five-year-old) was killed in an accident. She now spends all of her time praying for him in church, at his grave, etc. Meanwhile, the other five children have not only lost their brother, but their mother as well. What can I do to make her realize that the little boy is in heaven and her five other children need her?

A worried grandfather

Dear Worried Grandfather,

The loss of a child is a great sorrow to a mother. We should be patient and understanding, even if sometimes grief may seem excessive. However, your daughter's prolonged mourning is objectively excessive. Time heals, or at least soothes, the deepest wounds. By now your daughter should be able to carry on her duties to her family quite well.

Since you have been unable to assuage her grief, I would say that she needs medical help. It might be easiest to ask your priest for advice. He should be able to direct you to a suitable doctor who can provide the psychological and medical assistance that is called for. Or perhaps your own doctor might be best.

Meanwhile, comfort your daughter all you can and don't let anyone be unkind to her. She is obviously suffering very much and needs our sympathy. I am sure you have told her that her baby is with God—he was too young to imperil his soul by sin.

I would think that with proper professional help your daughter will be well quite soon. All of you have a promise of my prayers and a remembrance at Mass.

(April, 1975)

"STAND BY YOUR CROSS"

Dear Father,

My son was brought up as a Catholic. He also married in the Catholic Church. Before marriage his wife was Protestant and when they were married she converted to Catholicism.

They have been married eighteen years and have two teenage sons. The youngest, sixteen, has never received First Communion or Confirmation. The family has been gradually falling away from the Church.

During their marriage they have been unfaithful to each other, to the extent that now they are speaking of divorce.

My son is depressed and has resorted to drinking and living with another woman, and is very hostile toward God and the Church.

My son's wife has also been living with other men. Their teenage sons are following their example. I feel helpless because I cannot communicate with my son as he becomes very angry.

I am heartbroken and worried and very concerned about his soul.

I feel if my son would lead his family in the proper way, things may straighten out for them. Is there any way I can get him to listen?

For the love of our Lord Jesus Christ,

A worried mother

Dear Worried Mother,

The story you have to tell could be repeated, with variations, by many a worried mother. Human beings are weak, sinful, and have a nearly infinite capacity for making a mess of their lives. That is why our Lord died on a cross for us.

So my answer to you will have to be in terms of the cross and two mothers.

The first mother was Mary, the mother of Jesus and our mother. She saw her Son die abandoned and in pain, no sinner Himself, but carrying the burden of all men's sins. Her heart was pierced with sorrow, but she never turned away. She stood by the cross of Jesus.

The second mother was named Monica. She had an errant son who for years lived in sin, rejecting all her pleas. Since her son would not listen to her, Monica turned to God, and year in, year out, she besieged the Almighty for her boy. In time he did turn from his sins, so completely that today we know him as St. Augustine. And we know his mother as St. Monica.

Each of these mothers stood by her cross. It was heavy and brutally painful, but their conduct has been a shining example to sorrowing mothers ever since.

So, my advice to you, since your son will not listen to your pleas, is this: stand by your cross as Mary did, confident that Jesus is there, bleeding with you and ready to give His redeeming grace to any sinner. Pray to your heavenly Father for your son, as Monica did, patiently, endlessly, never giving up. God the Father and God the Son are all-merciful, and I think that they are especially merciful to heartbroken mothers.

So pray, try to keep the friendship of your son and his family, and leave the rest to God. Time heals, even though scars remain. And although you may not see the results of your prayers in this world, you will in the next. Be of good heart, worried mother. It is never too late, and it never will be.

(September, 1976)

PRAYER

WHY DO WE HAVE TO PRAY FOR SUCH A LONG TIME?

Dear Father,

In the Gospel we read that all those who asked Jesus to heal them of their illnesses or afflictions were granted their request in proportion to their faith. When asked by Jesus if they had faith, in some instances, to their affirmative reply, He cured or healed them. It was an on-the-spot cure. Why is it that when we pray, asking for temporal or spiritual graces, we have to pray for a long time before a request is granted? And yet Jesus said: "What is needed is faith." How is the faith of the Gospel people different from ours?

A puzzled reader

Dear Puzzled Reader,

The miracles of our Lord are very special, indeed unique, answers to prayer. His primary intention was to arouse and strengthen faith in Him and His mission. Those who asked Him for a cure had to have at least a disposition to faith as a preliminary condition to His on-the-spot cure. Then Christ worked the miracles recorded in the Gospels.

Times have changed since then. Our Lord has died and risen, and we know He is the Son of God. The special circumstances of His earthly life are now over and gone, and there is no longer the same need for miraculous answers to prayer as a sign of who He was and is.

This is not to say that miracles do not still occur. They do, but they are no longer needed in abundance as signs of Jesus' mission. Nonetheless, He has solemnly promised that if we ask we shall receive (Matthew 7:7), sometimes by a miraculous response, though this is rare, and more commonly by what we might call an everyday answer to prayer.

It is important to understand what is involved here. Our Lord will answer our prayers if we ask for something that is for our spiritual good, and if we ask with the right dispositions. One of the right dispositions is faith, either explicit or implicit, in God's word. We know that He has answered the prayers of His people in the past, so we implore Him for the same for ourselves.

The difficulty arises when we ask for temporal blessings, such as health, success, etc. Only God knows whether or not what we ask for is truly good for us. So, while we are certain that He always answers our prayers, sometimes His answer is "No." It is very hard for us to accept such an answer in a particular circumstance, but it is the only really kind response.

Our Lord's example in the Garden of Gethsemani (Matthew 26:39) shows us how we should pray. He asked His Father to free Him from the chalice of suffering, but, "Not my will, but yours, be done."

In other words, in a spirit of faith—and ours can be even greater than the faith of the Gospel people, because we know Christ is God—we make our petitions. If they are for our spiritual good, He will surely answer in the affirmative. If we ask for temporal blessings, He will give them to us if they are good for us, and He will refuse them if they are not.

Only a spirit of loving trust in God will allow us to accept His decisions patiently and tranquilly. For only He knows all things. Pray to Him with confidence, and thank Him for what He gives. For even a negative response is a loving gift of what is best for us. Your faith will let you see this, even if dimly.

(December, 1976)

PRAYING IN TONGUES

Dear Father,

Could you please tell me about "praying in tongues"? Though I feel no need nor attraction to the Charismatic Movement, I believe one should be informed about it. Wishing to learn about it, I sent for the Bishops' Guidelines which I read. I read nothing in them about "praying in tongues." Recently I visited a friend in our parish who is a charismatic. She told me that at times she prays privately "in tongues"; and that at the parish prayer group, those present will at times "pray in tongues."

Is "praying in tongues" a valid part of the Charismatic Movement? Just what should one expect attending a Charismatic Movement prayer group that would be following the Guidelines? Frankly, I am confused.

Sincerely yours,
An inquirer

Dear Inquirer,

Praying in tongues has been defined as speaking in one or more "languages" not learned by human means. The words do not make up a true language, but are sounds that must be interpreted by one who has the charism of interpretation.

Glossolalia (speaking in tongues) is referred to some twenty times in Luke and Paul, but the texts are very hard to interpret. After the days of the infant Church, Catholics made very little of the gift of tongues until a decade or so ago. Only now is serious research being undertaken. So, to begin with, let us be open to the action of the Holy Spirit, but careful to avoid possible dangers. We do not yet know enough to be certain.

Good Catholic charismatics say that praying in tongues is meant to make the one who prays more docile to the Spirit. They say that the gift of tongues is not a gift which enables one to prophesy. The message may be simply a prayer of praise or love.

On the basis of incomplete evidence, psychologists seem to think that those who speak in tongues, while perfectly sane and normal, do not manifest a conscious or produced speech; they pray in a pre-conceptual and non-objective way.

Some dangers are obvious. Some might consider speaking in tongues as a real language from God, miraculous or nearly so. One who possessed such a gift could easily consider himself so privileged that he alone would be the norm of truth. Needless to say, there is no Scriptural foundation for such an attitude.

The American Bishops, who have given the Charismatic Movement encouragement, said in a 1975 report: "Other aspects of the charismatic renewal which call for caution are such things as healing, prophecy, praying in tongues and the interpretation of tongues. It cannot be denied that such phenomena could be genuine manifestations of the Spirit. These things, however, must be carefully scrutinized and their importance, even if genuine, should not be exaggerated."

Pope Paul, also in 1975, spoke encouragingly to an International Conference of the Charismatic Renewal. He praised the movement and reminded its followers that all spiritual gifts need to be tested for orthodoxy by the hierarchy. The gifts most to be desired, he said, are those higher gifts most useful for the community, most of all charity, which alone makes the Christian holy.

Catholic charismatics, therefore, should keep in mind that the gift of tongues is the least of the gifts. It seems to help some very much in their nearness to God, which is good. But no such gift is comparable to the Mass or any other sacrament. In the last analysis, what we should all do is allow the Holy Spirit to act upon us as He sees fit, knowing all the while that any movement which turns us away from the Church cannot be from God.

Only time, study, experience and the prudent discernment of the hierarchy can untangle this rather mysterious experience. Let us await developments with confidence and serenity.

(June, 1978)

"MAY I PRAY THIS WAY?"

Dear Father,

What do you think of the practice of people saying to God, for example, "If you cure my child of this sickness, I promise to _____"? Is this bargaining with God? Shouldn't we do good works whether or not God answers our prayers in the way we want? It doesn't seem right that our prayers and good works should hinge on the results of whether or not our requests are answered. However, I can also see how a person can sincerely say to God: "If you grant me this wish, I will visit the sick in the hospital." Lots of good can come from these promises.

A concerned Christian

Dear Concerned Christian,

When our Lord taught us how to pray, He told us to ask for our daily bread, i.e., the things we need to love and serve Him well. If that is the case, we should confidently ask Him for the things close to our hearts. Sometimes, we want something so desperately that we are tempted to "bargain" with God, to promise something in exchange for the favor we want.

This approach is very human, and I am sure God understands the good will behind our craftiness, but the whole approach smacks too much of the market-place. Promises made in desperation may not be easy to keep. The only real bargain we should readily make with God is something like this: "Dear Lord, if what I ask is for the good of my soul, and if You grant it, I will try hard to love and serve You better."

The essential truth here is this: if you pray with the proper dispositions for something conducive to your salvation, your prayer will be answered. The rub is that we cannot be sure that what we ask for is really conducive to our salvation or to the salvation of a loved one.

Only God knows that. Jesus' prayer in the
Garden of Gethsemani was the perfect prayer
—He asked to be freed of the terrible chalice
offered Him, but, "not my will, but yours, be
done." Why? Because the will of God, our
Father, is always the very best thing for us,
even if we cannot see how at present. One day,
in heaven, we will see to our astonishment how
often God saved us from our own folly.

(April, 1974)

AM I OVERPRAYING?

Dear Father,

I sometimes assist at two Masses on Sun-
day. One of my friends recently discouraged
me from doing this. She said it was over-
praying—that is, by attending two Masses I
would not gain anything extra, and I even ran
the risk of having it become routine, thus
having less impact than if I just attended one
Mass. She said it was like repeating a prayer too
often, and that a prayer should be said less
often and thought about more.

A sincere worshiper

Dear Sincere Worshiper,

Each Mass gives God new glory and is the
occasion for God to grant to the Church the
fruits of Christ's redemption. Hence, each additional Mass means more praise to God and
more blessings for us.

Granted that general truth, some people are tempted to conclude that if one Mass is good, ten Masses are better. Not necessarily so. The Mass should be an opportunity to encounter Christ, according to our individual graces and capacities. God leads men in different ways. I know a holy old man who serves six or seven Masses every day, with devotion and great profit. But for most of us, the Church's wise pattern of Sunday Mass, and, when possible, daily Mass, is the norm.

Nonetheless, if you are so inclined, a second Mass on Sunday (or any other day) is by no means excessive. You will be able to judge whether or not your presence there is mere routine. It need not be, even though our human frailty exposes us to that possibility. It is the desire and intention that counts. A second Mass is not "over-praying," and it is false to say that you do not gain anything extra. You do, and very much.

So go to your extra Mass. You have a firm grasp on what matters, and you will be blessed.

(July-August, 1978)

HOW SHOULD WE RESPOND TO THE HOLY SPIRIT?

Dear Father,
    Could you please tell me about "being slain in the Holy Spirit"? I am attracted to the

Charismatic prayer meetings because of the love, joy, and peace I feel when attending. Like all searching Charismatics, I have attended other denominational prayer meetings where hundreds of people are fainting all over the place, and it is being called "slain in the Holy Spirit." There is a certain Catholic church here in this vicinity that is encouraging this type of action, and this has me confused.

Confused

Dear Confused,

"Slaying in the Spirit" refers to a phenomenon whereby the touch of one person causes another to swoon. Descriptions of the experience mention a floating effect, a feeling of peace and joy, and, somehow, the influence of the Holy Spirit.

Slaying in the Spirit seems to have been common at Protestant revival meetings of the past, and now it has been reported among some Catholics. Without making a final judgment, which will be up to the hierarchy after careful investigation, it is my opinion that we should look upon the phenomenon with great reserve. People may seek it for the wrong reasons—just for a thrill, for example. It may be induced, I suspect, by a kind of mob hysteria, which is anything but a true experience of the Holy Spirit.

If a Catholic wishes to respond to the Holy Spirit, let him do so in simplicity and quiet prayer. And let him judge the validity of his position by its fruits in peace, virtue, and fidelity to the Faith. Those who seek God in the extraordinary easily open themselves to a religion of the bizarre, which will never be satisfied by the simple faith-filled living which is God's ordinary will for us this side of heaven.

I would not urge Catholics to seek this experience because, always, one judges the extraordinary with caution.

(December, 1978)

ETHICS

IS "STRETCHING" THE RULES SOMETIMES OKAY?

Reverend Father,

I've been trying to straighten out in my own mind what is acceptable morality in ordinary business and social life today, and I'm really confused. I know the rules, so to speak, and I realize that even "good men" feel that there are some cases when they can be "stretched," when allowances can be made. In other words, in practical matters, most people seem to feel that you don't have to go by the exact letter of the law, as long as you don't get into serious, outright lying or dishonesty.

The movie—and before that, the book— All the President's Men *has really got me wondering about the above, however. Men who feel they have an important task to perform, can apparently feel justified in achieving their goals through means that are not "above board." How far has this spread in our way of life? What can the "ordinary" person do not to be infected by it? Where do you draw the line, without being scrupulous or unreasonable in your demands upon yourself or others?*

Let me give one small example: suppose I must fill out a form for a job that means everything to me and to my family's well-being. There is a question on it about my health and technically speaking, I should say, "Yes, I did have that illness." However, I am completely over it with no aftereffects, and if I admit that I had it, it will surely jeopardize my chances of getting the position. This is a computerized form with no room for any written explanations. What would you do, Father? What will I wish I had done when I stand before God?

This is the kind of thing that comes up in all our lives, over and over. When nothing important is at stake, it's easy to "apply the rules" strictly and put your conscience at ease. But it's when our mission in life is involved that it gets sticky....

Grateful for advice

Dear Grateful,

The demands of morality in business and social life are almost enough to confuse anyone. Business deals can be so complex that no rule of thumb is enough for guidance. One must know all the details, weigh them, and make an informed judgment working from the basics of the moral life, i.e., one may not lie, steal, defraud laborers, etc. The particular difficulty for men of good will lies, I think, in the business and political climate of our times. Recent disclosures of wholesale bribery, with vast sums involved, the use of lies and thievery for political ends, would seem to be only the exposed tip of the iceberg of corruption.

Throughout history, some men have always been persuaded that evil means are licit if the cause is good. The cause is commonly monetary gain, but it could be anything that serves a personal or social purpose. Nonetheless, evil may not be done that good may result. A good end does not justify an evil means. In short, it is not easy to be a good Christian, and virtue often means that one is going to suffer loss—financial, personal, political, social.

Sometimes the loss is only minor, but sometimes it can require a kind of heroism when the consequences are serious. I recall with pride a good doctor who told me that his Catholic conscience cost him about $40,000 a year, simply because he would not practice medicine contrary to God's law.

As regards the form you must fill out: a lie is the assertion of something I believe false in a context in which genuine communication is reasonably expected. Although lies are always wrong (and some gravely so), sometimes it is necessary to conceal the truth, as, for example, to keep a secret that should be kept. In the case you describe, if the questioner has a right to know about your past health problems because they will notably affect your job performance, you must admit you had the illness. If your medical history has no real bearing on the situation and honestly will not affect your work, you may answer the question in the negative. What you are really saying is, "No, I have had no illness that will affect my job qualifications."

This is a delicate matter, one which can be abused, as if a license to lie were being given. Not at all. The answer I suggest can be properly understood in the way I indicate, and, given a good reason for responding that way, it is licit. Let your honest conscience be your guide. Just be sure it is honest.

(July-August, 1976)

THE QUESTION
OF THE JUST PRICE

Dear Father,

I am a businessman. I have owned my business for approximately ten years. When I first started the business I would do whatever was required to obtain an order. After some years I have returned to the Church, made my confession, and try to be a daily communicant. To date, with the help of our Lady, I have managed to keep straight. However, I have one problem which is bothering me. How do you determine a fair price for your service? We have some customers (large firms) to whom we sell at lower rates than to the others.

A businessman

Dear Businessman,

Business ethics can be involved. The question of the just price, fortunately, is so basic that men have studied it for centuries. Here are some of the principles for arriving at a just price for commodities bought and sold on the open market:

A price, to be just, should represent the judgment of the general buying public on the value of the commodity. The judgment is reached in the open market, in the face of competition. The buyer, who knows the market, feels that he can and will pay the price asked, and the seller feels that he is getting a decent profit. If there is fair competition, prices that are too high (and hence unjust) will not be paid. Prices that are too low—below cost—are sometimes set in order to corner the market and be able to set higher prices in the future. This is unjust. A seller may lower his prices if he can do so because of his greater volume or efficiency.

A just price is not a static thing. It will range from a high to a low limit, and any price within this range will be just. A number of factors will determine a just high or a just low. If I sell in my immediate neighborhood, I can profitably set a price lower than the one which involves extensive packing and shipping to a distant buyer. Higher volume will allow a lower price than selling fewer items at greater handling costs.

So, as a general principle, the market price can be taken as just unless there is evidence to the contrary. The market price will vary, from high to low, depending on such factors as time, place, quantity and quality. In your case, I presume that your lower price for large firms is justified by volume or some other reasonable consideration. As long as the prices you ask are accepted by the men in the market, in the face of competition, the prices are just. A reasonable fluctuation between maximum and minimum is normal and morally acceptable.

I commend you for your fine Catholic conscience. Perhaps it may help you serve God in your vocation to reflect that businessmen are necessary servants of society. They perform an essential and honorable function. In your struggle to serve men (and consequently to serve God) morally and justly, try to look upon your business both as your own livelihood and your contribution to the welfare of your neighbor. We need each other. We cannot get along without each other. I wish you deep satisfaction and a clear conscience in your work.

(April, 1977)

WHAT IS "SITUATION ETHICS"?

Dear Father,
I had never heard of the "new morality" or "situation ethics" until I recently joined a study

*group. However, the correct nature of this is
still too obscure in my mind. It seems to be
quite a dangerous error. Is it?*

A bewildered Church-goer

Dear Bewildered Church-goer,

The "new morality" is old enough to have
been condemned by Pius XII in 1952.

Situation ethics holds that our moral decisions about right and wrong should no longer
be based on universal moral laws such as one
finds in the ten commandments, but on the
situation in which that problem occurs. Morality, in this system, depends upon a person's
evaluation of his circumstances, which are
unique, with little or no reference to an objective, binding natural law. Reflection alone will
then allow a judgment of conscience to suit the
situation; my subjective persuasion is enough,
without reference to any objective norm outside myself. The only requirement is that I be
sincere and conscientious in my judgment.

Situation ethics, like most errors, has a
kernel of truth. It attempts to apply new, and
good, insights of modern science about the
uniqueness of the person, moral culpability,
etc., to ethical problems. Unfortunately, it
stresses excessively, and very often exclusively,
two of the elements of human conduct which
determine morality, i.e., circumstances and
motive. There is a third element, ignored or
downgraded by situationists, namely, the ob-

ject itself, the thing with which an action is essentially concerned (stealing, for example).

Circumstances and motive can change and modify subjective culpability, but they can never eliminate the general law. Thus, if I take someone's life by accident, I am not guilty of strict murder, since circumstances and motive do not point to murder. But true murder is still forbidden. I can only decide the morality of an act if I have and know morally relevant values. These values are by nature general; their validity transcends any concrete situation. Situation ethics implicitly denies the obvious fact that certain actions are morally evil. They are so in themselves. The situationist rests everything on the person's good intention, independently of the action performed. But there can be no good intention unless there is a willingness to follow what is right, i.e., the moral law, which is independent of my private, subjective notions.

The new morality tends to discard all moral obligations. It equivalently wants to make man God, the only one who can determine what is right or wrong. It forgets that man is made free not to do what he pleases, but to obey God freely.

Situation ethics canonizes the view that apparent sinners may be very good people. Thus, they will say that fornication is quite all right if the pair love each other and mean no harm; the fact that fornication is evil is not really pertinent—all that matters is good will and "love."

Situation ethics is practiced by many people who never heard of the term. It is the ethical norm for large numbers of Americans who think that nothing much is really wrong as long as you feel that it isn't. Many Catholics, especially young ones, have been taken in by these views.

Yes, the "new morality" is quite a dangerous error. I hope this brief summary will help you to see why.

(April, 1978)

MISCELLANEOUS

"HE WANTS ME TO PROVE IT"

Dear Father,

This is my second year teaching religion to fifth graders. The first year the children really seemed to get a lot out of the class, and I had no problems. For example, when they asked how we can know there is a God, I told them we can know He exists because someone had to plan out the wonderful order in the world and universe—it couldn't just happen—and that thinking creatures like us had to be made by someone even more intelligent. And then I said that God Himself told us about Himself in the Bible.

Last year, the children believed all this and were satisfied, but this year one of the boys doesn't. No matter what I or the other children tell him, he says you can't know for certain that there's a God.

What do you suggest we do with this boy? He is very intelligent and it seems a pity that he is questioning his Faith so young. He is a leader, too, and I'm afraid he may lead other children astray.   *A concerned teacher*

Dear Concerned Teacher,

Your young philosopher, I feel sure, got his scepticism from some adult. Many people think that we can't prove a thing exists unless we can see it, weigh it, measure it, etc. They cannot follow abstract reasoning, even in its simplest elements, so they reject the perfectly sound argument you gave this boy, i.e., the argument from order in the universe.

We know that God can be known by supernatural faith in divine revelation, but the First Vatican Council defined that man can also know God through reason. Most of us are not professional philosophers, but the finger-prints of God in His creation are so visible that it is not hard to come to a knowledge of God's existence (cf. Wis. 13:5-9). St. Paul even says (Rom. 1:20) that those who do not reach God in this way are blameworthy.

All of us are helped by easier approaches than the metaphysical arguments. We know that men of all ages have believed in God. We know that our conscience constantly reminds us of moral law, and there cannot be a law without a lawgiver. We know that the sin and injustice of this world should be set straight some day—and this cannot be done by blind forces, but only by a Somebody. And we all have an ineradicable longing for happiness that only a God could satisfy.

Most of all, of course, we know Jesus Christ, who was man and also God. The readiest proof for the existence of God is there for anyone who reads the Bible with an open heart. God will make Himself known to me in faith and nobody will ever be able to prove to me that He doesn't exist.

Tell the young man some of these things, gently but firmly. Point out to him that a proof is perfectly good even if some people can't understand it. Most of all, let him know that since he has the Faith, he knows of God's existence by the highest of all certitudes. Finally, don't make a big issue of all this. We can hope that the boy will learn in time.

And keep on teaching the Faith. We *need* sound and dedicated Catholics to pass on our heritage. An occasional setback, or even a failure, should not deter you.

(April, 1974)

"WHAT HAPPENS TO ME?"

Dear Father,

I've heard the explanation of how suffering that is offered to God is not empty or useless.

I'm a young student lawyer, and I just lost a case. I'm convinced of the man's innocence, but we lost and he was convicted. I'm not mad at anyone; I don't blame the jury. They probably all acted exactly as they felt was right.

Now this man will go to jail. He'll have to suffer a lot of things: loss of reputation, family hardships, etc. If I say I believe that this can make him a better person if he knows how to accept it, and make him better before God and in eternity, then what happens to me?

I'm not sick, poor, condemned. I have no occasion to suffer. At the end, will that man in jail be a better person before God, will he be happier in eternity than me because he has suffered?

A Jewish student lawyer

Dear Friend,

I hope that all your life as a lawyer you never get used to injustice. You are beginning well. Stay that way.

The book of Genesis describes the ultimate cause of suffering. Our first parents, created by God in innocence and happiness, rebelled and brought upon themselves and their descendants suffering and death. This is the sad heritage of sin.

But what about *unjust* suffering, the suffering of the innocent? Is God a cruel God who delights in pain? Of course not. Nonetheless, we find it very difficult to explain the problem of suffering and evil. The books of Job and Ecclesiastes and some of the Psalms are helpful, and the first five chapters of the book of Wisdom shed a great ray of light by pointing out that justice, whether by way of reward or punishment, will certainly come in the next life, even if it does not in this world.

For Christians, the life of Jesus completes the response. His suffering, wholly vicarious, redeemed man. In order to share in His glory we believe that we must somehow share in His suffering also. We believe that our suffering benefits both ourselves and others. We can accept it as expiation if we are guilty of sin (and who isn't?), and in loving fortitude if we are innocent.

In short, God makes suffering serve a good purpose if we will let Him. If we have the will and courage to see our misery, to humble ourselves before our Maker, we can atone for our own sins and those of others. So if there is mystery here, there is no injustice, as St. Augustine emphasized.

There is no point in thinking that we can clear up all the mystery of suffering. But we do know that it is a consequence of original sin, that it can be (though we can never be certain) a penalty for personal sin, that it can be simply inexplicable, humanly. In the case of your jury, it would seem to be a matter of human frailty, which we cannot eliminate. Men make mistakes, and only God can undo some of them.

In this life, the all-good God sometimes sends us suffering for our profit, and sometimes He merely permits our pain. Come what may, we should try to accept our human condition. All men, except those who die as tiny babies, have some suffering, though some seem to have remarkably little and others far too much. The amount and kind of suffering we have is God's business. If He allows us to have much suffering, including injustice, He will give us the strength to bear it. If He gives us little, then we will be judged on that and on that alone.

So don't measure your virtue or heavenly reward by the sheer quantity of your suffering. What counts is the love and fortitude with which you manage the suffering God sends or permits in your life.

And keep in mind that there will come a day for every one of us when all tears will be wiped away. Meanwhile, let us trust God, who knows our hearts and will comfort us if we let Him.

(May, 1974)

"I TRIED TO TALK TO MY MOTHER...."

Dear Father,

I tried to talk to my mother one day about a problem, but she said she was too busy. I was always· kind of shy and never approached her before, just kind of worked out my own problems...but I wanted to talk to her. I tried again. This time she listened (I told her while she was ironing), but the only answer I got was, "For pity's sake, K..., don't be so immature."

The priest at Church is really great and really "in," but he's not the kind of person I would tell my problems to, and I don't know who else to go to.

How do you relate to parents? How do you make them understand a problem and make them realize it's not as little as it seems? How do you talk to them? Somewhere we're just not communicating.

Dear K...,

When you have a problem you should tell your mother very clearly that you need help. Perhaps she also is shy, or perhaps she needs to be reminded of her responsibility.

Sometimes you might want to approach someone else, not your mother. If your priest is really "in," why not talk to him in confession (I hope you go often)? There is a secrecy about confession that makes it easier to speak one's heart.

Keep in mind that you won't get help unless you look for it. This may be difficult at first, but you will have to break the ice yourself since other people don't even know that you have a problem. For your comfort, most of us had to go through this when we were about your age.

So talk to someone. Your mother is obviously the first one to approach, but anyone you trust will do, and I would urge you not to be afraid to ask the advice of a priest.

First, last and always tell your troubles to your Father in heaven. With His help and the help of some human being, you should find the direction you need and have a right to.

(January, 1975)

"WHOM SHOULD I TALK TO?"

Dear Father,

I would appreciate your advice in this problem. Two years ago, I befriended a young man who was discharged from Marine Corps (why?) and had many emotional problems. I extended to him the hand of friendship and our association developed into a fine camaraderie.

Then a year ago, he became a member of a motorcycle club and everything changed. Now he is aggressive and likes everything contrary to the principles of the Catholic Church.

Because he has a managerial position in a large corporation, he convinced a social worker to give him the role of foster parent for a boy of fifteen. I know that he is an unhealthy influence on this boy. He ridiculed me when I tried to talk to him about religion and going to church.

My question is: what should I do? My "friend's" parents are totally indifferent, and the aging aunt he lives with practically idolizes him. Whom should I talk to? Or should I just fade out and let Providence take over?

Please advise.

Worried

Dear Worried,

If this young man had many emotional problems and has now manifested a notable change in temperament and character, the wisest thing to do would be to tell the story to the social worker, who will surely want to investigate to see if your friend is not perhaps in need of some care himself. And, clearly, a decision should be made as to whether or not he is a suitable foster parent.

If you can manage it, I hope you will keep your association with the young man. Sooner or later he may respond to a faithful friendship, and eventually, in God's own time, he may be willing to listen to some advice about his religion. I suspect you have the stamina to hold out for the dawn of such a better day. Pray for him and try to be there if he needs you.

(March, 1975)

WHAT ABOUT CREMATION?

Dear Father,

I noticed in the magazine that readers can ask a competent theologian to give the Church's views on certain matters. I would appreciate receiving your views on the Catholic Church's stand on cremation. Having worked in an undertaking establishment (in a secretarial capacity), I was amazed at the cost of burying the dead.

Since our soul leaves the body at the moment of death, what difference does it make if we are cremated or buried in the ground?

One other thing I find difficult to understand: we are living in a changing world and the Church has made many changes, and I am sure as time goes on will make more. These changes are rarely ever discussed in sermons, and I think there is a great need for the people to understand the various changes that are being made and the reasons for these changes.

Would appreciate hearing from you.

Sincerely,

Dear...,

Christians have always buried their dead for two reasons: (1) our faith in the resurrection of the body, and (2) respect for the body as a member of Christ, a temple of the Holy Spirit.

Of course, cremation can in no way hinder our bodily resurrection, nor is it intrinsically a sign of disrespect for the body. Nonetheless, Christian instinct has always preferred burial. Many ancient peoples who practiced cremation have given it up, but there seems to be more interest recently among some Americans.

Recent Church legislation has liberalized considerably rules about cremation. Catholics may now choose to be cremated, unless they do so for reasons hostile to the Christian life, such as a desire to deny the sacredness of the body or the promise of resurrection.

Permission need not be requested any longer, and funeral rites may be carried out at the crematorium.

Despite this new freedom, it should be noted that the Church still prefers the custom of burial in imitation of the Lord. Further, we should discourage the practice of scattering the ashes over open water or the countryside.

I agree that priests should explain the legitimate changes made in Church life. Part of the turmoil in some parishes could be dissipated by sound instruction. It is also important for people to know that most things have *not* been changed, despite erroneous opinions to the contrary. The easiest example is contraception, which is still gravely forbidden by the law of God.

(May, 1975)

"HOW CAN I TELL THEM?"

Dear Father,

For some time now I have been convinced that I have a religious vocation; as a matter of fact, I have already decided on a particular teaching order, have spoken to the mother superior, and have spent some time at the convent, all of which have only served to strengthen my intention.

Everything seems to be going well—with one exception. I have not yet told my parents about my vocation. Once, half-jokingly, I told my mother that I might become a nun, and her reaction was so negative that I haven't dared speak of it since.

Her objections are strictly out of love: she sincerely believes that I'll be unhappy. And I,

for my part, have no wish to cause my parents
any pain, for I love them both very much.
    How can I tell them?
    Thank you in advance, Father.

                            Chosen by the Lord

Dear Friend,

    According to Church law (Canon 538),
any Catholic who has the proper qualifications
may be admitted to religious life. Parents may
not hinder a true vocation, whether to the convent or the seminary.

    One of the basic natural rights of human
beings is the right to follow one's own vocation.
This does not mean that a young person may do
as she pleases out of mere whim or caprice.
Picking a vocation demands serious reflection,
prayer, advice and self-evaluation. Sometimes,
with all the good will in the world, a boy or girl
will decide on a vocation for which they are
manifestly unfitted. Sometimes parents will
know better than the child what necessary
talents are lacking for a given vocation.

    However, assuming that a vocation to
religious life is present, parents may not stand
in the way. Minors may be wise to wait until
they attain legal majority, but it is licit, possible and perhaps good for them to enter earlier.
What is required is some good advice (from
mother superior or a prudent priest) that will
fit the situation. Perhaps filial love will suggest

waiting a while. Perhaps you will decide that no matter what the pain, you must follow your vocation now.

How can you tell them about this? Simply by telling them, gently and lovingly. There is no magic formula that will take away the pain for you or them. You will have to face up to the difficulty.

It may comfort you to know that you are not alone—this situation is rather common. And it is a mystery. Why should parents object if Christ is calling their daughter to be His bride?

Keep praying. I pray that your vocation comes true.

(December, 1975)

"AM I OBLIGED TO HELP?"

Reverend Father,

I would like to know what we, as Christians, are morally bound to do with regard to accident victims. I am naturally one who would want to rush to help anyone in need—at the site of a car accident, for example, or when someone has collapsed on the street. But you read so many things these days about people who went to help someone and were taken in, that is, they became victims of a criminal hoax.

A wonderful man I knew stopped to help an apparently sick woman who had two small children with her. It was on a rather deserted street. No sooner had he gotten out of the car than two men jumped out from bushes and leaped on him. They beat him, took his money and left him in serious condition. He was a long time in the hospital and barely managed to survive the ordeal.

My fears have reached the point that I don't know if I would dare to risk everything to help someone in similar conditions. Also, the sight of blood just paralyzes me, and I think I would be useless. Still, if I were the only one at the scene of an accident, what would be my obligation?

Sincere Inquirer

Dear Sincere Inquirer,

Your question is one no one would have asked, I suspect, just a few years ago. But today it is very real.

The key to the answer is this: we are bound to love both ourselves and our neighbor. The problem is to reconcile those two loves in certain difficult situations.

We are all bound to have reasonable care for our own welfare, not out of mere selfishness, but out of genuine love for the precious thing we are because of creation and redemption. But our neighbor is also a precious creature for the same reasons. Our obligation to help him in his need is commensurate with his need and our own, as also with our means and op-portunities. In other words, I should help when I can.

Except in extreme necessity, I am not strictly obliged to help another at the risk of serious physical harm, unless, of course, I have a special duty, as a mother to her child or a parish priest to his flock.

We can't eliminate all danger from life, but we should not normally leap into danger-ous situations. It is a fact that in emergencies we can often do things we would have thought beyond our strength. But we must be unselfish-ly realistic by keeping in mind that no one is held to what is morally impossible for him.

All of this, of course, is general principle. It does not take into account the total self-emptying of the saint or the hero.

My suggestion for action in a potentially dangerous situation is this: perhaps the best thing to do would be to speed away and call help. In practice, only your own swift, honest judgment at the moment will tell you what to do. Do it without qualms. In a dangerous back alley, charity might tell you to go *get* help, not give it. I would not fault you for that decision.

(March, 1976)

YES, GOD EXISTS!

Dear Father,
    Are there any proofs for the claim that God's existence is 100% certain?
                                        Faithful Catholic

Dear Faithful Catholic,
    You are asking the most basic of all philosophical questions. The First Vatican Council solemnly declared that God can be known by reason, but long before that men, Christian and non-Christian, elaborated proofs of varying kinds. The most famous, perhaps, are the five ways of demonstrating God's existence worked out by St. Thomas Aquinas.
    Thomas works from sense experience that are effects, as it develops, of God. In other words, we go back from effects to their cause. These classic proofs are complicated and philosophical, too complicated to outline profitably here. Let me give a hint of the drift, at least, of one proof, the proof from order:
    The world of nature shows a marvelous order. Rain freshens the earth and brings forth crops; acorns have the innate potency to grow into oaks, etc. But order demands intelligence. It cannot be just blind, because order means arranging things according to a plan, which only a mind can conceive. Hence, there is an intelligent Being behind all this order and one who works always, twenty-four hours a day for all time. We call this intelligent Being God.

All these proofs start from a fact of experience—change, imperfection, finality, etc., and they all point to the existence of a Being which is the ultimate cause or explanation of the human experience. It is important to note that advances in science cannot invalidate these proofs because the point at issue is philosophical, and its solution rests on metaphysical principles not open to change. Hence anyone who denies God's existence because of science is trying to answer a philosophical question in the manner of physical science—and this can't be done.

It is important to realize that not all men are capable of the philosophical reasoning which leads to a sound knowledge of God. Man *can* reason to God's existence, but not all men are able to do so. Many men don't think much or accurately, and all of us are hindered by prejudice, emotion, pleasure, the cares of this world and plain carelessness.

We know from history that those who have reasoned to God's existence have often come to an idea of God that was distorted and partially untrue. God Himself has solved this problem for us by revealing clearly and accurately not only mysteries, but also truths that we can struggle to by reason.

We do, then, have a 100% certainty of God's existence. If we work it out by reason, fine. If we do not, then we have God's revelation of Himself which we know by faith, the highest of all certitudes. Reason and the external world bear witness to God, but the best witness of all is God Himself, who has revealed Himself to us finally in Christ, our Lord.

(June, 1976)

THE RIGHT APPROACH

Dear Father,

I have been beset by constant visits from representatives of a religion not my own who are extremely insistent both as to their method of approach and their obvious knowledge of Bible sources. In the beginning I used to listen to their reasonings and try to explain the truths of my Faith to oppose their counter-attacks. Now I am tempted and do close the door as soon as I realize they've come again. I've always learned that faith is a free assent to what God has revealed through Christ and His Church, and as I cannot force faith on another, so another should not force faith on me. Do you think the attitude I've taken of late might be the solution, or would you suggest another approach? Is ignoring these people the easy way out or the more courageous stand which is really an act of charity toward myself and my family?

A hesitant housewife

Dear Hesitant Housewife,

I once had visitors like the ones you describe. But they never came back after the second visit because I turned their Bible quotes back on them. My aunt, bothered by repeated recruiting of this sort, ended it all by hitting one of the pair with a frying pan.

I don't recommend either approach, least of all the frying-pan-ploy. There is little or no hope of changing the mind of someone bent on converting you, so I would say that it is best to avoid argumentation with people of this kind. Their minds are made up and closed, and their biblical expertise is usually superficial. At any rate, few Catholics are equipped to argue fine points of Scripture, and it is a fact that some simple Catholics have been persuaded by such proselytizers to abandon their most precious possession, the Faith.

You have a right to your privacy and the undisturbed profession of your faith. So, without hesitation, lock your door and firmly but courteously keep these unwanted visitors out. Simply have nothing to do with them.

Obviously, I do not at all approve of the methods used by your visitors. But I do admire their zeal to spread their religion. If only Catholics, without being equally obnoxious, were equally zealous to spread the Faith!

(May, 1977)

PRINCIPLES WILL ALWAYS REMAIN, APPLICATIONS MAY CHANGE

Dear Father,

Could you please clarify for me why we are now allowed to eat meat on Fridays unless it is Lent? I do not understand why it used to be wrong to do so, and now it is not.

I would like to know if things like the following were ever really declared outdated: genuflections in church, use of holy water, covering of women's heads in church, and other various ways of publicly showing our faith.

A bewildered Catholic

Dear Bewildered Catholic,

In order to understand the answer to your question we must first realize that there are (1) principles, and (2) applications of the principles.

The principles do not change but the applications may. For example, it is a basic principle of Christianity that we must do some penance. This is fundamental and will never change. One application of that principle is the very ancient practice of fast and abstinence. Is it essential that our penance be expressed this way? No. The Church has from the very beginning urged this kind of penance, and often made it obligatory, as she has the right to do. But since conditions vary so much around the world, the actual practice, e.g., of Friday abstinence, varied considerably. The pattern we were accustomed to in the United States until recent years was found to be impractical as a general law. So the Church has changed the application but has kept the principle. We are still bound to penance, but the way we apply that obligation through fast and abstinence has been changed.

Another principle tells us that we must show God reverence and worship, and that we need to do this through external signs of our faith. We apply this principle in various ways, such as the use of genuflections, holy water, etc.

The principle will always remain, but the applications may change. Genuflection, for example, has long been our customary gesture of adoration, but the early Christians made a profound bow rather than a genuflection. It was not until the sixteenth century that genuflections were used in the Mass. They are still used, and they are still the ordinary sign of adoration before the Blessed Sacrament.

Holy water, a sacramental and symbol of purification and washing, reminds us that we should be reverent before God and try to preserve our baptismal innocence. It has not been declared outmoded in the Church.

Women prayed with their heads covered in the time of the early Church. It was not a matter of divine law but a custom (cf. 1 Cor. 11:16). The custom was kept for centuries, but, since it is not a matter of obligation, in recent times it has fallen into disuse in some places.

The ways in which we manifest our faith publicly can, therefore, change with the times if the Church decides a change or modification is called for. Customs and tastes change. It is hard to change old habits, hard to realize that much-loved practices are not essential to a living faith. All the same, we *need* the symbolic and satisfying gestures which remind us and others of the faith that is in us. It is a sad abuse for Catholics to stroll about the Church without any sign of reverence to the Blessed Sacrament. We can still abstain as now required in Lent, even if the requirements are much more lenient than in the past. Holy water, ashes on Ash Wednesday, all the blessings that sanctify the various occasions of life are precious parts of our Catholic life. They may vary somewhat in different centuries, but they are part of the sign language of the faith and they will always be there.

(September, 1977)

QUESTION JOURNALISM
IF IT'S NOT RESPONSIBLE

Reverend Father,

More and more I am noticing that our Catholic newspaper is becoming too liberal and earthly. The last editorial, in defense against criticism, stated: "To avoid tensions, readers must outgrow the tendency to view everything in a Catholic newspaper as the official position. We are free (outside of faith and morals) to present a variety of legitimate Catholic positions on human relations and the social order. A major task is to bridge the gap which so often separates Christian teaching from everyday life." I fear that our paper has too little of the official position and too many so-called "Catholic" positions to justify the publication being called Catholic.

As much as I wish to keep informed of our local Church news, would it be best to discontinue subscribing to such a misleading paper (perhaps even informing the editor of reasons for my decision)? What ways can the ordinary lay person use to correct the local abuse of sound, stimulating journalism? Is a subscription to L'Osservatore Romano *the best substitute for missing Catholic news?*

Thanks for your answers.

A concerned Catholic

Dear Concerned Catholic,

Since Vatican II the Catholic press (newspapers and magazines) in the United States has splintered into unhappy segments. Some publications—perhaps most—have been fairly sane, balanced, and so helpful for the upbuilding of the Body of Christ. Some few have been so stridently liberal as almost to merit the label of anti-Catholic. Some conservative publications are so out of touch as to be nearly benighted, and they have wrought almost as much harm as the illiberal liberal press.

The Church needs a good press. We need to know the truth, even when it displeases us. Most of all, we need to know the truth of the Faith. Catholic journalists have an important and very difficult task. Unfortunately, not all journalists are able to meet the demands of their craft, either by reason of poor judgment or plain ignorance.

I think that the time has come for readers of the press to meet their own responsibilities by questioning journalism that is not responsible. We should not be harsh or hateful in our criticism, but our editors should be kept on their toes if they misrepresent or underplay sound Catholic doctrine.

All the same, apart from clear doctrine, there are many areas in which journals can and should present informed opinions. There are, as your newspaper sensibly notes, a variety of legitimate Catholic positions in a number of areas. Unfortunately, many Catholics seem to assume that there is only one Catholic position on every possible problem. Even more unfortunately, not all Catholics are able to distinguish what *must* be held from what *may* be held. The key responsibility for accurate teaching in this area lies with the press itself. And they should be called to order if they print what is truly untenable.

Stay with your diocesan paper. If you can afford it, the English edition of *L'Osservatore Romano** makes good and profitable reading. I never miss it.

(October, 1978)

ABOUT APPARITIONS

Dear Father,

I have always been devoted to our Lady and have tried to comply with her requests to recite the rosary daily. I try to explain to my best friend who is caught up with some "popular" (but unapproved by the local bishop) apparitions that we are not expected to follow any visionary unless the Church approves. She just tells me, however, that our Lady is very

* 1 Year Subscription to L'Osservatore Romano
$34.00 air mail (comes weekly)
write to: Daughters of St. Paul
2105 Ontario St. (at Prospect Ave.)
Cleveland, Ohio 44115

*hurt by this indifference to her "latest ap-
pearances." How can I best explain this point
to her?*

An earnest devotee of our Lady

Dear Devotee of our Lady,

A supernatural vision is a charism through
which an individual perceives some object that
is naturally invisible to man. Visions which are
not supernatural are illusions or hallucinations
caused by pathological mental states or dia-
bolical influence. And, of course, the pur-
ported vision may be plain fraud.

When a "vision" is proposed to Catholics
for communal action—processions, new forms
of devotion, etc.—the Church must step in to
make a decision as to authenticity. Between
1931 and 1950, of twenty-two so-called Marian
apparitions, only two were approved. The
Church must be very cautious. She does hold
that there are genuine private revelations, such
as Lourdes and Fatima, but there are also
frauds and illusions masquerading as the real
thing. Most apparitions, as a matter of fact, are
not approved, and even when they are approved (as in the cases of Fatima, Guadalupe,
Knock, LaSalette, Lourdes) the Church never
uses her authority to impose on us belief in the
apparitions, but merely authorizes a pious
belief.

We should never give to apparitions subsequent to those expressly attested to in the Bible

any exaggerated importance, even when there is every reason to believe them authentic. Some personalities, unfortunately, are drawn in unhealthy fashion to make visions the very center of their spiritual lives, even to the point of disobedience to Church authority.

Some unapproved apparitions of our Lady are Garabandal (Spain); Necedah, Wisconsin; and Bayside, Queens, New York. Catholics should have nothing to do with them.

Approved apparitions, on the other hand, can assist us very much to develop a deeper love of the Gospel, sorrow for sin, a spirit of reparation and other basic Christian attitudes.

If your local bishop has not approved of the apparitions you mention, you can be sure that our Lady is not "very hurt" by indifference to them. Can anyone conceive of our Lady's promoting disobedience to the Church, which speaks for her Son?

I cannot say how much success you will have convincing your friend that she should abandon this false devotion. Some devotees of such apparitions often end up in blind, unreasoning, stubborn disobedience. They simply will not listen. Speak to her gently but firmly, and, above all, commend her to the intercession of our Lady, for whom she protests devotion. Sooner or later, we may hope, she will come to true, not false, light.

(June, 1979)

A SENSE
OF PRIORITIES

Dear Father,

What are the regulations concerning the frequency of the reception of the Eucharist? If I go to Mass on Saturday evening to fulfill my Sunday obligation and receive Communion at this Mass, and then on Sunday unexpectedly have the opportunity to attend another Mass, may I also receive Holy Communion at this Mass?

I also have another question, for I work in a Catholic store, and for about a year or so there has been a great demand for the pyx for special ministers. Recently I noticed that a new style features enamel inside the pyx. To be liturgically correct, should the pyx, like the chalice and ciborium, be gold plated inside? I understand that the new liturgy allows now non-beeswax candles for Mass and the sanctuary lamp. But, out of respect for the Body and Blood of Christ, isn't it improper for the sacred vessels to be without gold plating?

It has also bothered me immensely that in some churches, the Bible has been given a place of honor and the Tabernacle relegated to some corner. It's true, the Word of God is living, but the Word made flesh is present in our Catholic churches. I can always read and reverence the

Bible in my home, etc., but I genuflect and worship the Body and Blood of Christ at church.

What can we Catholics do to remedy a situation which appears to lack a sense of priorities, a feeling of distraction, a wrong shift in values?

Thank you for your advice in these matters.

A layman

Dear Sir,

There are several situations in which we may receive Communion more than once on the same day. After going to Mass and Communion, one may also receive at a later Mass celebrated for a funeral, wedding, First Communion, ordination, etc. You may receive Saturday evening and again on Sunday—two different days are involved.

The *General Instruction of the Roman Missal*, nos. 289-295, gives the new rules for sacred vessels. They should be "made from solid materials which are considered suitable in each region. The Conference of Bishops will be the judge in this matter.... Chalices and other vessels which are intended to hold the Blood of the Lord should have a cup of non-absorbent material.... Vessels which are intended to hold hosts...may be made of other materials which are locally considered valuable and appropriate for sacred use.... Vessels made from metal should ordinarily be gilded on the inside if the metal is one that oxidizes; gilding is not necessary if the metal is precious and does not oxidize."

As you can see, gold plating is no longer always necessary. The bishops determine what is suitable for sacred vessels and also for the makeup of candles for Mass and the sanctuary lamp. The whole idea is to make it easier to use local materials which are beautiful and reverent.

Christ is present at Mass in a number of ways: in the congregation, in His Sacred Word of Scripture, in the person of the minister, and, finally and most especially, in the Holy Eucharist. For the reservation of the Eucharist outside Mass, the *General Instruction* mentioned above (no. 276) says: "It is highly recommended that the Holy Eucharist be reserved in a chapel suitable for private adoration and prayer. If this is impossible because of the structure of the church or local custom, it should be kept on an altar or other place in the church that is prominent and properly decorated."

The Blessed Sacrament should not be relegated to "some corner." It deserves, if possible, a special chapel, and at very least, a place of beauty and prominence. There need not be and should not be any difficulty about the presence of Christ in His Word and in His Real Presence. The latter Presence is unique, altogether singular. It can in no way be equated to a book, even the greatest Book.

If we prepare for the Blessed Sacrament a proper place of reservation, there need be no difficulty about giving the book of the Scriptures some prominence of its own, but it should be clearly less than that given to the Blessed Sacrament. In many churches it is not easy to set aside an ideal place for the reservation of the Blessed Sacrament, but, however imperfect, the place is the very center of things in the church, and nothing should be allowed to overshadow it.

If you think that there are abuses along these lines, you have the right to complain to your bishop or the diocesan liturgical commission.

(September, 1979)

ONE MEDIATOR?

Dear Father,
If the Bible states that there is one Mediator between God and men, why do Catholics pray to the Virgin and the saints? I also think it is quite improper to pray to Mother Thecla. Please explain your reasons to me.
A devotee of the Bible

Dear Devotee,
"We have but one Mediator, as we know from the words of the Apostle: 'For there is one God, and one Mediator between God and men,

himself man, Christ Jesus, who gave himself as ransom for all' (1 Tim. 2:5-6). The maternal duty of Mary toward men in no way obscures or diminishes this unique mediation of Christ, but rather shows its power. For all the saving influences of the Blessed Virgin on men originate, not from some inner necessity, but from the divine pleasure. They flow forth from the superabundance of the merits of Christ, rest on His mediation, depend entirely on it, and draw all their power from it. In no way do they impede the immediate union of the faithful with Christ. Rather, they foster this union."

This quotation from Vatican II (*Dogmatic Constitution on the Church*, no. 60) clearly stresses the Catholic Church's teaching that Christ is the unique Mediator between God and men, without denying that we may and should seek also the secondary mediation of the Blessed Virgin (and other saints). A little background is necessary to understand this.

Scripture does not explicitly refer to the veneration and invocation of saints, but gives a principle out of which Church teaching and practice developed. Holy Writ allows veneration of angels because of their dignity and union with God—cf. Joshua 5:14; Daniel 8:17; Matthew 18:10. Since the saints are also immediately joined to God (cf. 1 Cor. 13:12; 1 Jn. 3:2), it follows that they, too, are worthy of veneration. The book of Revelation (5:8; 8:3)

THE FIFTH RULE:

You have taken yourself too seriously.

assumes that we may invoke the intercession of the angels and saints.

It is quite clear that from the early days of Christianity, saints were honored and prayed to. The faithful saw no problem, since the same inspired Scripture which asserted clearly that Christ was the unique Mediator also clearly taught us to ask the prayers of our brethren (cf. James 5:16-18; Romans 15:30). St. Paul, as we know, constantly asked the brethren to pray for him. If we may legitimately ask the prayers of our own in this life, obviously we may ask them to intercede for us when they are in God's presence after death.

So, when the Blessed Virgin or the blessed in heaven intercede for us before God, their intercession is secondary and wholly subordinate to the one mediatorship of Christ, and its efficacy rests on *His* redemptive merits. Their prayers for us have meaning and force only through Jesus Christ.

To God we give absolute worship, and the only perfect Mediator between God and man is Christ. We venerate the saints, but we do not worship them. To God we pray, "Have mercy on us." To the saints we pray, "Ask God to have mercy on us."

Mother Thecla Merlo lived a very holy life. We have every right to beg her intercession before God, and, in so doing, look only to the ultimate mediation of the Lord she loved so much.   (October, 1979)

A SUNDAY CATHOLIC?

Dear Father,
    Isn't it better to be sincere with God, praying at home, and worshiping God in my heart than to be a Sunday Catholic, who is hypocritical Monday through Saturday?
                                        A businessman

Dear Businessman,
    I assume that you refer to the kind of Catholic who goes to Mass on Sunday and lives the rest of the week more or less as a pagan. Such people exist, unfortunately, and they do great harm by their bad example.
    However, if you want to avoid being a hypocrite, don't become another kind of sinner! For that is what you would do if you decided to stay away from Sunday Mass and pray at home. By doing that you would not be sincere with God, as you desire to be, since God asks of you that you worship Him publicly on Sundays, at Mass. The private prayer you offer at home is splendid, but on Sundays and holydays public participation in the Holy Eucharist is required of us. We do not solve one problem (that of the hypocritical "Sunday Catholic") by creating another (that of the man who prays only at home to be sure he is not a hypocrite).
    The bad example given by the Sunday Catholic who is a weekday pagan can easily

tempt us to think that fidelity in the face of fakery is too much to ask. What use is the Church if there are so many bad Catholics? What good is Mass if people don't profit from it?

We need to reflect that we are all sinners, all in need of God's mercy. But millions of Catholics around the world, few of them suspected of high sanctity, gather faithfully around the altar every Sunday, and despite their weekday sins, try hard to love God and neighbor. We should be there with them, not at home despising their frailties.

As for the poor hypocrite—better a "Sunday Catholic" than no Catholic at all. The poor soul may be desperately seeking strength to improve. At any rate, he is doing one great thing right. Pray for him and all the rest of us sinners, including yourself.

(December, 1979)

THE ECUMENICAL MOVEMENT

Dear Father,
How can I help the ecumenical movement without imposing my beliefs on my friends and neighbors?

An ordinary Catholic mother

Dear Ordinary Catholic Mother,

There are many things you can do. Some suggestions:

Join with our separated brethren in prayer, when that is possible. Your diocese will have guidelines to follow, I am sure. Perhaps your area promotes the annual (January 18-25) Week of Prayer for Christian Unity. At any rate, pray regularly that we may all be one—this is the basic irreplaceable, ecumenical activity.

If you can, join with your non-Catholic neighbors in works for the common good. Working together out of love for God and man quickly breaks down senseless barriers.

Try hard to eliminate from your thoughts, words and actions anything that is not scrupulously fair to our non-Catholic friends. Harsh judgments about other Christians were common in the recent past; they should be rejected, not merely for political reasons, but because in so many cases they were false. It is hard to want to be united with someone you scorn or despise. Happily, there is no objective reason to scorn or despise other Christians. To know them is almost always to love them. Let us be sure we never drive anyone away from the truth by cruel words or actions fathered by cruel thoughts.

If you can manage it, have the courage to speak about religious matters. Don't wait for something "ecumenical" to happen. Make it happen, by simple, friendly talk about ordinary things. These days it is very easy—all we have to say is, "What do you think of our new Pope?" This will give you a chance, perhaps, to explain a bit of what we believe and to manifest an interest in what others hold.

Above all, be a good Catholic. No amount of learning, worldly wisdom or charm can match the sheer attraction of goodness. Your manner of life will say more to others about the riches of Catholicism than mountains of words. If your non-Catholic brethren can see from your life that you love God and love them, you will have brought us much closer to the unity that God wills for all.

(January, 1980)

BECOMING A SAINT?

Dear Father,
I've heard the expression regarding the saints that "If they could do it, I can do it too." But, as a father of a family, I haven't been able to do much to deepen my spiritual life on a day-to-day basis, and I would appreciate a few practical pointers about how to begin and how to continue. Becoming a saint sounds kind of impossible to me without recourse to extraordinary means out of my reach.

Sincerely,
A despondent dad

Dear Despondent Dad:

It surprises many Catholics to hear that all of us are called to holiness. The Second Vatican Council devoted a whole chapter (Ch. V, *Lumen gentium*, nos. 39-42) to the universal call to holiness, and long before Vatican II, revelation itself (cf. v.g., Lk. 10:27) taught us again and again that God's design for us is to be holy as He is holy.

What is at issue is not a special call for special people, but a command, an obligation, for all of us. We are to love God with our "whole" heart, soul, strength and mind, and our neighbor as ourself (Lk. 10:27). This is a frightening command—"kind of impossible," as you say—at first hearing. But God never commands the impossible. Holiness, quite simply, is what He wants us to attain, and what He will help us to attain.

The first, essential level of holiness is to possess sanctifying grace, i.e., to share in the supernatural life of God. Merely hanging on to sanctifying grace and avoiding serious sin is not enough, however. God wants us to go as far as possible, according to our graces and state in life, towards a deeper and richer love of God and neighbor. We must aim at a more perfect union of our wills with God's will, because if we love Him we will keep His commandments.

Growth in holiness is worked out in the concrete details of one's life. Fathers and mothers do not have the same chance for prayer that a Trappist will have—and they are not expected to try to live like Trappists. They are expected to pray the best they can, according to the possibilities of their life. The short prayer of a busy father is just as good as the long prayer of a devoted Trappist—because each gives to God what God asks. Neither is expected to be somebody else.

Concrete suggestions could go on for pages, but here are a few: be sure to pray every day, any way that helps. Most of all, if you can, get to Mass and Communion often, besides Sundays and holydays of obligation. Look upon the joys and sorrows of each day as God's loving hand on you—reach out and accept it. Help the poor, even to the point of hurting. Try to witness to Christ, by word and action. Meditate on God's Word, and be ready for Him to speak to you through Scripture and the liturgy. Try to live in the spirit of the beatitudes (Mt. 5:3-10). Be ready for the cross that will be put on your shoulder. Be detached from the greedy pursuit of wealth. Make "Thy will be done" the prayer of your life.

Most of all, in simplicity and serenity, do the best you can to cooperate with the graces God gives you. If your heart is open to the love of God and neighbor, you will grow in holiness and, as a consequence, happiness. No extraordinary means are necessary. Just use the life you have as the father of a family—it is filled with opportunities for love of God and your most important neighbors, your own wife and children. So one becomes, as we all should, the very image of the Lord (2 Cor. 3:18).

(March, 1980)

FIRST CONFESSION AND FIRST COMMUNION

Dear Father,

I am a father whose concern has deepened through the years for the catechetical instruction of my children. I do not feel that they are being taught the Catholic Faith in its entirety, but some vague theories on brotherhood and self-growth.

My youngest child is going to be receiving First Communion soon. She has not, however, made her First Penance, and according to the parish custom, will not make her confession for another couple of years. I know that the Pope has spoken out for First Penance preceding First Communion. What is my obligation as a parent with regard to my children's catechetical instruction? And can I do anything about getting my child to the sacrament of Penance before she receives our Lord in the Eucharist? She has not yet even been taught anything about the Real Presence, and I have my doubts as to whether this doctrine will be treated at all. A puzzled parent

Dear Puzzled Parent,

It is unfortunately true that some catechetical programs do not teach children the whole Faith, or even a reasonable facsimile thereof. At this point, parents must assert their own primary right and responsibility to see to their children's Catholic education. Teach them yourself, if necessary, or put them in the hands of a teacher you trust. For the sake of the common good, I would urge you to protest the inadequacies of your local catechetical program, perhaps even to the bishop himself. Be courteous but firm. Handing on the Faith to the next generation is an absolutely basic duty of adults; we should not merely wring our hands if it is not being done. Charitable but effective action is called for.

Your parish "custom" should bring itself into agreement with the current obligatory practice of the Church, which says that in all but quite rare cases, a child who has reached the use of reason should receive the sacraments of Penance and Holy Communion—and in the normally proper order, i.e., confession before Communion. Your parish seems to be clinging to experiments formerly allowed but now discontinued and abrogated. The experiments were based on the idea, as far as I can see, that because a child of seven is unlikely to commit mortal sin he need not go to confession; further, confession and Communion are distinct sacraments, and children need to learn that they need not always go together.

The difficulties cited did not need extreme measures to bring out the truth. A child can be quite clearly taught that Penance and the Eucharist are distinct. To do this successfully it is not necessary to postpone his first confession for months or years. Careful instruction, too, can easily point out that confessions of devotion (confessions of venial sins only) are just as helpful for youngsters as for adults. It is quite true that no one is bound to go to confession unless he is guilty of serious sin, but this sacrament is not reserved for serious sin only. All of us need the grace, the guidance, and the inspiration to be derived from confessions of devotion. The little child, in particular, needs to be taught to go to confession as a regular part of his spiritual life. It would be tragic if youngsters were brought up thinking that they should approach the sacrament of Reconciliation only when absolutely necessary. There are ominous indications that, in practice, we are raising such a generation today.

If you judge that your daughter is ready for First Penance, either prepare her yourself or get someone you trust to do so. Check with a priest who knows her, and when she is ready and willing, arrange to have her receive, with you nearby, if possible. No one need know that this wonderful occasion is taking place, but the child at the age of reason has the *right* to receive both Penance and Communion. It is really a ridiculous and unjust discrimination to say that a child can go to Communion but may not make a first confession, although quite prepared to do so.

When children are young, we can teach them the need to approach the Eucharist worthily. This attitude, we can hope, will stay with them all their lives, and should give them a greater esteem for confession and a greater readiness to go to confession often. Today the Church is trying to renew our appreciation of the sacrament of Penance—can this be done without teaching the young its importance, not just as an emergency measure for the spiritually dead, but as a beloved commonplace of the life of grace? The Church, obviously, does not think so. She wants first confession and First Communion to go together, and we should obey.

One last point: perhaps the best way to teach your children the importance of confession is to go often yourself. Parents teach best of all by their example.

(April, 1980)

THE "ULTIMATE ESCAPE"?

Dear Father,
    I have a friend in his final year of philosophy. He says he cannot see how God can fit into

any thinking person's serious idea of life. As far as he's concerned, all people spend their lives escaping, and God is the ultimate escape. How can I convince him otherwise?

A concerned friend

Dear Concerned Friend,

I will try to give your philosopher friend a few leads which may, I hope, convince him that he is being less than philosophical in thinking of God as the "ultimate escape." What I say may be pretty murky to most readers, but it should be intelligible to the young philosopher.

The existence of God is known from Revelation, but there are purely human, non-revealed arguments for His existence, drawn from: the principle of causality; the contingency of man and all in the universe; man's awareness of moral responsibility; the persistent and widespread belief in God.

In other words, there are philosophical grounds for asserting that God exists. Even Kant, who rejected the traditional demonstrations of God's existence, insisted on keeping God as a postulate in the moral order of practical reason. Classical philosophers have accepted the existence of God as an innate idea (Descartes), an intellectual intuition (Malebranche), the result of the spontaneous judgment of reason (Aquinas).

In more recent times, many question whether non-empirical language can carry any meaning at all, and here, precisely, lies the problem (for them) of knowing God. How can talk about God refer to a Transcendent really existing outside consciousness? Tackling the question from reason alone would be the following: Hartshorne, Malcolm, Whitehead, John Cobb, Jr., Wisdom, Flew, Richmond.

Approaching more closely the classical Protestant reliance on faith alone are those who try to work from both reason and faith. Followers of American Empiricism have broadened the notion of experience to include faith, which offers answers to ultimate questions. Phenomenology can see human existence as so clearly contingent as to require God as necessary. In a purely symbolic knowledge God is seen not as Cause but as Presence (Gilkey, Dupré).

Modern personalist and existentialist philosophers try to develop proofs for God's existence through reflection on the person and consciousness.

In sum, many contemporary thinkers affirm a transcendent God. They do not see, I suspect, how any thinking person can have a serious idea of life *without* God. The question, "Does God exist?" is the most fundamental of all questions. The answer is not transparently clear to the human mind, but it is not so mysterious that only faith can make it known. Speaking philosophically, to say that God exists is to give a response to a metaphysical question.

Physical science tells us *what* things are. The idea of God is always a *why*—it tells us why things are what they are, and why they exist at all.

All the same, metaphysics can go only so far in speaking of God. Where metaphysics ends, religion begins. The earnest searcher for truth (which is what the philosopher is), helped by grace, can come to realize that He who is the God of the philosophers is the God of Abraham, Isaac and Jacob, and the God of the Christians.

The human mind can offer the most stubborn resistance to unwelcome ideas. To accept God when one has up to now rejected Him would well be a trial. To refuse Him could well be nothing but an attempt to escape the Ultimate. Perhaps the best advice you might give your philosopher friend is that he read the poem "The Hound of Heaven," by Francis Thompson. Any respectable anthology will have it. It says a great deal about spending one's life escaping.   (May, 1980)

The Ideal Children's Catholic Magazine!

MY FRIEND

Now at last there is a special magazine
just for children ages 6-10.

32 pages in full color packed with enjoy-
ment, adventure, learning and inspiration.

MY FRIEND

will provide hours of happy
reading for *your* youngsters or students.

- Bible Stories
- Lives of the saints
- A Message
  from the Pope
- Poems
- Cartoons
- Contests
- Projects
- Science
- Songs
- and much more!
- comes out every month (except July and August)

$4.00 for 1 year; $7.50 for 2 years; $10.00 for 3 years.
For Canada: $4.50 for 1 year; Foreign Countries: $5.00

SPECIAL OFFER:
Bulk rates (5 or more copies) 30¢ (retail 40¢ per copy)

Send subscriptions to: **My Friend**
50 St. Paul's Ave., Jamaica Plain, Boston, MA 02130

Basic Catechism With Scripture Quotations
Daughters of St. Paul

This concise, direct book presents the fundamentals of the Catholic Faith in a question-and-answer format with related scriptural quotations.

Thoroughly indexed for ready reference, it is a vital handbook for everyone desiring to deepen or clarify his belief. 207 pages

cloth $3.00; paper $1.50 — RA0007

Morality Today—The Bible in My Life
Daughters of St. Paul

A unique way to study the Ten Commandments! In simple and clear language, but with a very personal approach, each commandment is explained in all its aspects, negative and positive. We are invited to ponder...adore...and speak to God, so that through instruction, reflection and prayer we may understand and love His holy Law.

All will find this book both informative and inspirational. 157 pages

cloth $3.00; paper $1.95 — SC0088

Spiritual Life in the Bible
Daughters of St. Paul

A volume which pursues the truth about a wealth of timely and fundamental subjects.

Written in a form of dialogue, the author continually draws from the book of books—the Bible—whose author is God, the Author of Truth and the true Light of the World.

A book which will be of interest to both those who believe in objective truth, and those who honestly seek to pursue the truth. 456 pages

cloth $5.95; paper $4.00 — SC0445

Living the Catholic Faith Today
Most Rev. John F. Whealon, STD, SSL, DD

This short volume packs a wealth of insights on practicing the Catholic faith now. Among many topics—Why believe in God; Why be a Roman Catholic; Ideas on parish life; Practical Ideas on Confession; How should a Catholic live the faith. A book to be owned by every Catholic adult and inquirer into the faith. 130 pages

cloth $2.50; paper $1.50 — RA0130

Why a Gift on Sunday?
Rev. John M. Scott, S.J.

"Why go to Mass?" In an effort to catch the wonder and fascination of what has been called "the most beautiful thing this side of heaven," the author provides compelling reasons and insights. The Mass is our gift to God and His gift to us.

148 pages

cloth $2.95; paper $1.95 — RA0210

Lifetime of Love
S.L. Hart

The practical problems of everyday family living. Backed by the sound doctrine of Vatican II. Covers the whole span of married life—from the day of the wedding until "sunset." Newlyweds, in-laws, the budget, raising children, sex instruction for little ones, divorce, birth control, family cooperation, the role of mother and father, teenagers, growing old together—these and countless more topics in this complete, up-to-date marriage manual.

534 pages

cloth $5.95 — MS0350

Questions and Answers for Our Times
Daughters of St. Paul

Questions proposed and solutions given! The authoritative voice of the Church providing clear answers to today's key moral problems. This important pamphlet includes the Pastoral Letter on Archbishop Lefebvre and Sexuality Study by His Eminence, Humberto Cardinal Medeiros. Also: Questions and answers on sexual ethics and many wide-spread evils. 29 pages

15¢ — PM1550

Religion in the Modern World
John Joseph Cardinal Carberry

"Some reflections on a topic which is extremely vibrant, popular, and, at the same time, confused and subjected to the influences of many diverse philosophies." 24 pages

10¢ — PM1600

A Right To Know Religious and Moral Values
John Cardinal Krol

A timely pamphlet on a topic that powerfully affects our eternal destiny. 26 pages

30¢ — PM1650

Daughters of St. Paul

IN MASSACHUSETTS
   50 St. Paul's Ave. Jamaica Plain, Boston, MA 02130;
     617-522-8911; 617-522-0875;
   172 Tremont Street, Boston, MA 02111; **617-426-5464;**
     617-426-4230
IN NEW YORK
   78 Fort Place, Staten Island, NY 10301; **212-447-5071**
   59 East 43rd Street, New York, NY 10017; **212-986-7580**
   7 State Street, New York, NY 10004; **212-447-5071**
   625 East 187th Street, Bronx, NY 10458; **212-584-0440**
   525 Main Street, Buffalo, NY 14203; **716-847-6044**
IN NEW JERSEY
   Hudson Mall — Route 440 and Communipaw Ave.,
     Jersey City, NJ 07304; **201-433-7740**
IN CONNECTICUT
   202 Fairfield Ave., Bridgeport, CT 06604; **203-335-9913**
IN OHIO
   2105 Ontario St. (at Prospect Ave.), Cleveland, OH 44115; **216-621-9427**
   25 E. Eighth Street, Cincinnati, OH 45202; **513-721-4838**
IN PENNSYLVANIA
   1719 Chestnut Street, Philadelphia, PA 19103; **215-568-2638**
IN FLORIDA
   2700 Biscayne Blvd., Miami, FL 33137; **305-573-1618**
IN LOUISIANA
   4403 Veterans Memorial Blvd., Metairie, LA 70002; **504-887-7631;**
     504-887-0113
   1800 South Acadian Thruway, P.O. Box 2028, Baton Rouge, LA 70821
     504-343-4057; 504-343-3814
IN MISSOURI
   1001 Pine Street (at North 10th), St. Louis, MO 63101; **314-621-0346;**
     314-231-1034
IN ILLINOIS
   172 North Michigan Ave., Chicago, IL 60601; **312-346-4228**
IN TEXAS
   114 Main Plaza, San Antonio, TX 78205; **512-224-8101**
IN CALIFORNIA
   1570 Fifth Avenue, San Diego, CA 92101; **714-232-1442**
   46 Geary Street, San Francisco, CA 94108; **415-781-5180**
IN HAWAII
   1143 Bishop Street, Honolulu, HI 96813; **808-521-2731**
IN ALASKA
   750 West 5th Avenue, Anchorage AK 99501; **907-272-8183**
IN CANADA
   3022 Dufferin Street, Toronto 395, Ontario, Canada
IN ENGLAND
   57, Kensington Church Street, London W. 8, England
IN AUSTRALIA
   58 Abbotsford Rd., Homebush, N.S.W., Sydney 2140, Australia